STREET LEVEL PRAYER

Loving Your Community Through Prayer Outreach

TODD W. VOLKER

Cover by Joel A. Volker

ISBN: 978-1-9810-4161-9

Dedication

To my bride, Pam. Thank you for living out the "for better for worse, for richer or for poorer, in sickness and in health" part of the deal with me for more than three decades. Here's to three more!

Table of Contents

PART 3: TOOLS

Introduction

I'm sitting in a folding chair under a pop-up canopy on a dirt lot next to a very busy street across from a hospital in Corona, California. I'm alone and wondering what in the world I'm doing there. Hanging from the canopy is a large, hand-made sign that says in big letters "Need Prayer?" No one has stopped by my booth today for prayer, and I'm thinking that it's been about two months of being here every week on Thursdays, and this might not be such a great idea after all. Was I really directed to do this by God? Did He really tell me to do this every week? I've had the chance to pray for a few people each week, but it feels weird to be sitting here with that sign up! People passing by must think I'm a nut.

Down the sidewalk I noticed a side-by-side tandem bicycle coming toward me. There is an older gentleman and a younger boy, who looks about 10 years-old, pedaling it. The boy gets off the bike and comes over to where I am sitting. He says, "Can you come over and pray for my grandfather?" The boy's name is Sebastian, and he explains that his grandfather, Fidel, has just been diagnosed with stage-4 prostate cancer. The cancer has already spread to his lungs and brain. He also tells me that Fidel doesn't speak much English, but that he will translate what I say into Spanish for his grandfather.

I go over to the bike and introduce myself to Fidel, and ask if he indeed wants me to pray for him. He consents, so I ask that the Lord bring His Kingdom right here for Fidel. I pray for healing and then tell his body to come under obedience to Christ, and for all abnormal cell growth to stop. I ask Jesus to take the cancer from

Fidel's body and to bless him with health. The exchange lasts less than two minutes, and during that time I don't sense anything unusual in my spirit as I pray. (I am simply praying out of obedience and in faith – with a confidence that God is good and wants to bring life and the gifts of the Kingdom for His children.) I then ask Sebastian to question his grandfather what was happening while I was praying for him. He reports that Fidel felt heat go through his body, from the top of his head all the way down to his feet. That sounds good, but there is nothing left to do at this point, so after thanking me Sebastian climbs back into the bike and they ride off.

About three weeks later I'm sitting in my usual spot there on a Thursday afternoon, and I see the same tandem bike coming down the sidewalk. Sebastian and Fidel both get off the bike this time and come over to the "Need Prayer?" Booth. They have big smiles on their faces. Sebastian reports that Fidel has had a full body PET scan, and that there is no sign of any cancer! We hug in a circle, and all I can say is "Jesus did that!" I drive home that day thinking about my journey and how I had ended up on that street praying for somebody with cancer. God had blessed me to be able to witness a miracle, and my heart is so full of joy that I weep.

That day changed me, and I knew without a doubt I was right where I was supposed to be. I sensed the Lord say to me "You were made for this." About two months later, Sebastian and Fidel came back again and reported that Fidel had a blood test (cancer antigen 125) that showed no signs of cancer in his body. Fidel told the priest at his local Catholic church, and the priest told the whole parish that God had healed Fidel from cancer. I tell people that setting up the "Need Prayer?" Booth is like going fishing: Some days you catch some, and some days you catch none, and once in a while you bring in a whopper. That day was a whopper!

The Purpose of the Book

The reason I wrote this little book is to encourage followers of Jesus to take His love and power outside the walls of the church building into the streets and marketplace. The idea of a "Need Prayer?" Booth is only one of a multitude of creative ways God is giving to His people to do outreach. I know I don't have the corner on the market of outreach. The ideas and principles in this book can translate into different forms of ministry "outside the walls." The point is to find the one that works for you in your context and go for it! This is what it means for the "the church to leave the building."

I want to say right from the outset that I have an agenda: to transfer an ethos of loving people the way Jesus loves them into doing outreach. *Our goal should be that people experience the love of God when we encounter them on the street.* That happens when we treat them with care and respect. If we really love people, and they in turn experience the love of God in that relational exchange, then we have won! Not everyone we pray for is healed, and not all with a request get their prayer answered in the way they were hoping. But it is my conviction that every time we pray with people, something good does happen, and that good begins with the love of God exhibited. That is the whole key!

This book is organized into three sections:

Part 1: TRAINING. This is a "how to" of sorts recounting what I have learned, much of it in the "school of hard knocks." I share it to give you a leg up in starting a public prayer ministry yourself. Not that I am an expert; after praying for thousands of people on the streets over the last seven years I am still learning about how the Holy Spirit moves and how to best engage people. What I do know is when we pray for others we must stay humble and acknowledge we are totally dependent on the Holy Spirit to bring the Kingdom of God. I want to give away this style of street ministry so others can join in the joy of seeing people touched by the love and power of Jesus when the church leaves the building.

Part 2: TESTIMONIES. These are a few of the stories of what God did in the Prayer Booth ministry. The purpose of sharing these "highlights" is to inspire you, the reader, to actually go out and do something like this. It is also to give God glory in recalling what He has done, and to build up a trust and confidence in you that He desires to do even more through you. God is not looking for Christian superstars, but simply friends who will say "yes" to His call and go with Him into the highways and byways. Jesus said His followers would see "greater works [miracles] than these" (Jn. 14:12), and such are waiting for you to share with Him as you go. My prayer is that many will read through this book and then step into the great adventure of following Jesus into ministry on the streets and in the marketplace.

Part 3: TOOLS. If you decide to do a "Need Prayer?" Booth, this section will give you the "nuts and bolts" details and some "do's and don'ts." It is a summary of some of what is discussed in Part 1, with some practical advice on how to get going in this specific ministry. Appendix A will give you a list of what you need for a "Need Prayer?" Booth kit.

PART 1

TRAINING

Chapter 1

IN THE BEGINNING – HOW I GOT STARTED

Many, many years ago I had a dream. This was one of those dreams that leave you with no doubt it was from God. In the dream I was going to my first day at work. I showed up at a bakery to learn the trade of a baker. The old baker was already there, and it was clear by looking at him that he had been at his work since the early morning. He was covered with flour from head to toe, and he was perspiring. He greeted me, and I told him I was ready to learn to be a baker. He looked me in the eye with intensity and said the most unexpected thing: "Your job is to pray!" I woke up with a very profound sense of the Lord's presence. Up to this point in my life I had been involved in one type of prayer ministry or another, including intercession, for several years, but this dream set me on a new direction in my ministry. I became more focused on prayer and read many books on the subject. Much of my prayer ministry became directed in praying and ministering to others, specifically in the different realms of healing. Little did I know that this would set the course for much of my life.

After teaching in the public school for about 23 years, the Lord called me to leave that profession and go into ministry. I didn't really know what "ministry" would mean, but it was clear that I was to get some training and give myself to that full time. One of my assignments in seminary was to spend a week living among the poor. I didn't want to do that because it was way out of my comfort zone. I suggested some alternative assignments to my professor, Dr. Bill Jackson, but he insisted I stick with the program. The only thing that helped take some of the fear away was that he said he was going to accompany me. We left the Inland Empire and drove to a ministry in the inner-city called the City of Refuge. It was a community of Jesus followers who lived in one of the poorest urban centers. They fed, clothed, and loved the homeless and poor of the community.

Each day Jax (Dr. Jackson), Steve Halligan and I went with others in teams into the neighborhood and into the streets. We brought breakfast to homeless in the morning and just spent time with them, building relationships. We delivered food to shut-ins in the late morning and then set up tables with groceries outside the poorest elementary school in the city in the afternoon. This was so that parents could pick up food after they picked up their children from their classrooms. Then in the early evening we helped distribute clothes and blankets to all who came to the ministry base. The whole time I felt very uncomfortable and awkward. Yet in the midst of this, God was chipping away at my heart, and I could feel more of His compassion for the people on the street. I still had lots of questions about the theology and practice of effectively helping the poor in a holistic (complete) way, but I knew that God was calling me in some manner to minister on the street.

Two events from that trip impacted me in a profound and life-changing way. The first was going out at night to bring a blanket and food to a disabled homeless man living behind an abandoned warehouse. He was camped out in a cardboard box, where the street lights didn't penetrate. He asked us if we were Christians, and when we said yes, he laughed and said he had been praying that God would bring him some fellowship. He didn't want the food or blanket, but he wanted to sing with us! We spent the next 20 minutes worshiping Jesus in that dark place, and as we all sang, the presence of God came in a way that I had never experienced before in a church. I was literally stunned by the encounter we had with Jesus there. It was amazing to feel the tangible glory of God while sitting on cardboard next to an old shopping cart!

The second event occurred the night before we finished our week at the City of Refuge. We had a time of prayer with this small community, when David, the leader of this ministry, got down on the floor and washed my feet. He took off my shoes and socks and then put my feet in a basin with water. As he was doing this, something inside me broke, and all I could do was sob. All the events of the past week came flooding back: God was imparting something through this leader to me in a symbolic, yet literal way. My heart was changed, and I knew God had given me a commission to serve Him on the streets. I still had no idea what that might look like!

Several months later, I was reading the newspaper at breakfast and came across an article about Shawn Heggi in Redlands who put out an A-frame sign by his truck in a dirt lot across from a hospital that simply said, "Need Prayer?" As I read the story about how people stopped and he prayed for them, I sensed the Holy Spirit saying to me, "You can do that." It was a way for me to minister on the street without being weird! The people would come to me, and I could use my gifts and calling for prayer to bless and help others in street ministry. I told my friend Luc Jackson (Jax's oldest son) about this idea, and he found a dirt lot across the street from Corona Regional Hospital to try the idea out. I got a pop-up shelter and some home-made signs that said, "Need Prayer?" and set out for a great adventure.

When you try to follow God in obedience, it will often be tested right away. The first person we prayed for was a demonized homeless man who kept coming over for prayer but would run away after about one minute of prayer. He would come back ten minutes later and then run away again. It was as if there was turmoil inside him between getting help and the evil spirit that wanted to keep him bound. This happened about five times, and I began to think, "What have I got myself into? Do I really want to do this?"

About three weeks later I set the booth up again in the same location, and after praying for several people, I sensed the Lord directing me to be consistent and return every week at the same time. I was usually by myself at first, as most of the people I told about this outreach thought it was a great idea, but weren't interested in helping me. After about four months, God sent me

Steve Collins as a partner in ministry, and over the next 15 months of being there every week on that dirt lot across from the hospital, we saw miracles! Many were healed and some found salvation in Christ.

About three months into this first location I saw Jesus heal Fidel from stage 4 prostate cancer. It was at this point that I knew I was on to something special. God was really showing up, and people were being touched by the love and power of Jesus. I expanded into a second weekly location in Riverside and then others took the vision and ran with it, too. I do realize that this is not the only way to do outreach in the street; God is the author of creativity, and He is giving the church new and effective ways to reach out into the community all the time. This is just one way, and I do not claim to have invented it. But it is a way to bring the Kingdom of God to the street and marketplace. Now, after over seven years, it feels like we are just getting started and this history is still being written. It all started with a dream, and I can say now that my real job is to pray.

Chapter 2

DON'T LET YOUR FEAR WIN

Sometime in the late 80s a major Christian ministry decided to use the *Jesus* film as a tool to introduce Christ to a wider audience. The strategy was to go door to door and give a VHS tape of the movie away as a starting point for the gospel. This was a very successful endeavor by all accounts, and our church at the time was involved in the project. I was very nervous about participating, but took my friend Tim Barrett, who is gifted as an evangelist, with me into our assigned neighborhood to knock on doors. I was very fearful, so I let Tim do all the talking at the first several houses. He would say, "Hi, I'm Tim and this is my friend, Todd, and we would like to give you this free major motion picture called *Jesus*. You may have heard of it." Then he would go on with his conversation. All was going well until it came for my turn to do the talking at the next house. I can remember panic hitting me as I rang the doorbell, and sweat was already appearing on my body. I was so nervous and fearful that when a woman answered the door I said, "Hi, I'm Todd and this is my wife, Pam, and we would like to give you this major motion picture called *Jesus*. You may have heard of it." I can't remember anything else that happened, but the woman looked very confused. I had no idea what I had just said. It was all a blur. But when we were leaving, Tim was laughing and when I asked him why, he said, "Bro, you just told that lady that I was

17

your wife, Pam! She must have been wondering what kind of church we are from!"

I think it is normal for most of us to feel somewhat fearful when we are trying to minister to people outside the walls of the church. The key is to overcome that fear by letting the perfect love of God become greater than our fear (1 Jn. 4.18). When I first started the "Need Prayer?" Booth several years ago, I was, for the most part, on my own and way out of my comfort zone. Every time I would set up the booth there was a voice in my head saying "What are you doing out here? You look crazy, and people think you are weird." Part of that was my own pride, and part was Satan trying to scare me. I had to just push through it because I knew that God loves me and had called me to do this ministry. The strong sense of calling to that ministry kept me going forward, and I was learning to lean on the safety of His love. Eventually that voice went away and the fear started to abate. But to be perfectly honest, I never feel totally comfortable when I am doing street and marketplace ministry. I still to this day feel that there is a tension, and I think that is because we are bringing the Kingdom of God into conflict with the kingdom of darkness. That creates a tension. The way God has wired each of us differently causes us to feel that tension in different environments and situations. It's not the same for everyone, and some feel fine knocking on doors and sharing the gospel. Others, like me, still find it horrifying.

I have a friend who has been a missionary to Muslims in North Africa for over 25 years. He has been in many dangerous situations as he has witnessed for Christ in hostile environments. When Libya had open borders at the fall of Kadafi, there was a short window of opportunity, so he went in with a team to evangelize and give away the same *Jesus* film in Arabic. This was a very unstable country at the time, and the team was arrested and detained before being miraculously released. I met with him a few years ago when he and his wife were on furlough. When I shared what I was doing he told me that he could never do something like the "Need Prayer?" Booth here in the U.S. because that would be way out of his comfort zone! That shocked me until I realized that God has made us to feel spiritual tension in different ways. Some are fine with going up to strangers in the mall and asking them if they know Jesus. That is not me! But there is a way to bring the love and power of Jesus to people outside the walls of the church that fits you. There will be a tension, yet we don't have to let the fear win. The perfect love of God can drive that out!

Chapter 3

LOVE IS THE KEY THAT OPENS HEARTS

If you have ever seen the musical or the movie *Oliver!* you may have noticed the big sign in the orphans' workhouse proclaiming "God is Love." One of my 15 minutes of childhood fame was being cast in the title role of this musical as a ten year-old in my elementary school. I recall wondering about this sign at the time when they were putting together the theatrical sets. It seemed out of place and ironic, as the orphans in the story were treated with anything but God's love. I think Dickens knew that there was a big difference between talking about God's love and actually demonstrating it in action, and he was playing on this irony. He knew that Christians often talk about the love of God, yet much of our interactions with other humans will not reflect His nature.

It is true that God is love (1Jn. 4.8), and this is one of the defining attributes of His character. If our goal is for people to experience God when we pray for them on the street or in the marketplace, and it should be, then they must experience love. We can never lose sight of this. When Paul is taking the church in Corinth to task about its use of spiritual gifts, he emphasizes the importance of love, making it preeminent above prophecy, faith and even martyrdom (1Cor.13)! He states that without loving people, all that other powerful activity is worthless. You may be so powerful in your prophetic ministry that "you can fathom all mysteries and all knowledge," but if people are not experiencing love from your interaction with them, you have accomplished nothing. I like the way Kevin Prosch says it in a line of a song: "Love is the key that makes it all work."

So it would seem to follow that we want to love the people we interact with in the street and marketplace. It is helpful to remember that love is a relational verb. One way we can show this love is by receiving people where they are, listening well while we demonstrate grace and empathy, and then praying in a relational manner. This might seem obvious, and a "given" for Christians to love, yet sometimes the interaction we have with others can be devoid of love. I have seen it many times, as well-meaning Christians attempt to minister to people on the street: a lack of love is conveyed through their words and actions. A typical example is where we are trying to "fix" a person by telling him all the things he needs to do. You can tell you are in your "parent voice" when you are using phrases like, "You need to..." or "You should..." This is often about correcting behavior, and getting the individual to start living better. But that can come across corrective and un-loving, even if our intention is to help. You may see clearly areas of sin and many bad choices that a person is making, yet in our context of prayer, we don't counsel and we try not to give advice. "You need to read your Bible every day" or "You need to pray regularly" might be good advice, but it usually conveys judgment and correction, not love. Our goal is for the individual to encounter the love of God, and that initial contact should be full of acceptance and grace. This does not mean we are approving of negative behavior, but we are trusting that God will "clean up" a person as God draws him or her near.

I have also observed the tendency of some believers to get pushy or preachy with people as well. Quoting lots of Bible verses and using church language is a sure way to come across as religious and un-loving. I have found it best to listen to people, use compassion and empathy, and then move into prayer as quickly as possible. I use scripture in my prayer (more on this later), but it flows out of a heart that wants the hearer to experience God's love and presence. If sin needs to be confronted, the Holy Spirit will do the convicting. It is God's kindness that leads people to repentance (Rom. 2.4). Again, we convey the love of God best by accepting people where they are, listening to their story, demonstrating grace and empathy, and then praying for them in a relational manner. With many we encounter on the street, this alone may be enough to open their hearts to the love of God.

I mentioned my friend Steve Collins earlier, but I want to tell you more about how Steve got involved in doing this ministry. I was teaching a class on prayer at church and was sharing some of the things I was learning by doing the prayer booth ministry. I had been going consistently for about three months every week, and most of the time it was alone. Steve came up to me after the class and asked if he could come out to the prayer booth and observe me. I said "sure" and he showed up the next day at my spot on 9th and Main in Corona across from the hospital. And he showed up every week and was never late. I found out that he had just retired after 40 years of working for the Santa Fe Railroad, and when you work for the railroad you must be on time!

Steve was very hesitant to get involved in prayer and it took some time for me to convince him that he could do it. One day, after about a month of staffing the booth together, he confided that he felt very inadequate because he was not well educated and had trouble in school with reading and writing. At that moment I felt God was giving me a nudge to help Steve out of the "nest." I said, "Ok, can you read that sign?" He said, "Yes, it says 'Need Prayer?'" I said, "Does it say you need to read and write well?" He said "No, just pray." I said, "Well you are qualified because I know you can do that!" He cried and I cried and that was a breakthrough for Steve.

I started making excuses to leave him there in the booth alone for an hour so he would have to pray for people on his own. I would say, "Steve, I need to do some shopping down the street and I'll be back soon." The first time I did that a cop pulled into the empty lot and Steve thought the guy was going to kick him off the lot. But the cop rolled down the window and asked Steve to pray for his marriage. He did it just like I had showed him, and he was very excited to share that with me when I got back from my "shopping excursion."

The more we prayed for people the more I saw that God had given Steve a heart of love for everyone we met. People really experience God's love through Steve, and he loves to hug them! I now refer to him as "God's Teddy Bear" because of the way he makes people feel comfortable and safe. He may not have all the education and training that I have, but he has the most important qualification for doing this ministry: He really loves Jesus and he loves people in a tangible way. He is the epitome of the kind of person we need in this ministry.

After about six months of the two of us working together in ministry twice a week (I started another booth in Riverside on Fridays soon after), Steve and I started to talk about him starting a prayer booth ministry in his hometown of Colton. I helped him set it up and it wasn't long before he and his wife Jenny were doing three prayer booths a week (at three different locations). He has in turn trained others to do this and the ministry continues as he loves the people God sends him. (I will discuss multiplication and team ministry more in a later chapter.)

Chapter 4

HOW TO PRAY THE LOVE OF GOD

I have lived in California all my life, yet I can only speak a few words in Spanish. Yes I know, it's a little ethnocentric of me to not expand my linguistic skills, but I have never really pursued learning another language. So when I have been in environments where Spanish is being spoken, it causes me to feel like an outsider. I feel intimidated and somewhat anxious. The same thing can happen in street ministry when we talk to people and pray in church language. That would be any insider lingo that includes terms or phrases that we don't use in a normal conversation. "Oh Lord of Hosts, let thy Shekinah glory rest on this sinner so that they will see the error of their ways, for Thou art omnipotent and inscrutable in Thy habitation" is not a prayer that will make any sense to most people you encounter on the street! This is a bit of an exaggeration, yet many of the terms and phrases we use as believers will most likely cause an unchurched person to feel like an outsider.

We are attempting to communicate love to the individuals we pray for on the street and in the marketplace so that they will be open to the work of God. Again, our goal is to show this love by listening well and accepting people where they are without being pushy, preachy or religious. Here I want to detail how to include the love of God in the actual prayer exchange. The first idea is to pray in a relational style that the recipient can connect with and understand. We want the person to feel included, not excluded. Regardless of whether the person is a follower of Jesus, I want to avoid using church language in the prayer. I keep my voice at the same volume and pitch as when I was speaking to the individual, and I keep the prayer short (one minute or less). The content of the prayer I use stays basically the same, with the exception of any prayer request the individual might have, or any revelation I receive from the Lord (more on prophecy later). The content is focused around the love of God.

The reason for this is simple, yet profound: The basic human need is to be loved! We are praying that they experience the one thing they want and need above all others: to be loved by God! This is what they were made for, so we are connecting them to the love of the Creator. I use the basic idea of the Father's love and affirmation of the Son in His baptism in the Jordan by John (See Mat. 3). The Father says to Jesus, "You are my son (identity), I love you (belonging), and I delight in you all the time (purpose)." This is what every one of us is looking for! This is the family we have been searching for all of our lives. We are inviting others into what one scholar called "the Holy hug of the Trinity."

If I am praying for Susan and she wants prayer for a job, my initial prayer would be something like this: "Lord, I thank you that you love Susan and brought her here for prayer today. Would you bless her by providing a job that will meet her needs? I thank you that Susan is your daughter, that you love her, and that you are delighted in her. Thank you that your love for her is so great that nothing can separate her from that love that is in Christ Jesus. Bless her family, her neighborhood, and those that she loves. Let her experience your love right now, right here in this moment. I pray this in Jesus' Name, Amen." Notice the emphasis on love in the prayer. I mention love six times in a 30 second prayer. It never ceases to amaze me how quickly and powerfully God can touch a person in such a brief prayer. I have come to believe that the Kingdom of God always comes in some manner when we pray like this. Sometimes it is visibly evident, and sometimes not, but the Kingdom always comes.

Many people, both in and out of the church, have this nagging feeling that God is mad at them. They feel that they are in trouble with God, and fear that He wants to judge and punish them. This view of God is more common than you might think. When we pray the love of God over people, that false image of God begins to lose its power over them, and their heart starts to open up to a loving and merciful Savior. Yes, it is true that our sin separates us from Him, but it is His kindness that leads us to repentance (Rom. 2.4). It grieves my heart, and I think it grieves the Holy Spirit, when I see well-meaning Christians outside sporting events and other large gatherings with signs that say, in effect: "Sinner, you are going to burn in eternal hell if you don't repent and believe in Jesus." There may be some truth in that, yet I would estimate that they are not winning a lot of converts with this approach. They are certainly turning many off to the gospel message, which is a loving God coming to earth in the person of Jesus to seek and save those that are lost.

Is there a better way? How about showing people love and respect, and demonstrating a loving God by the way we interact with them in our conversation and prayers? Most people already know they are sinners, and they fear a wrathful God. When we show them His kindness that leads to repentance, they will find that God has put all of His wrath for sin upon His Son at the cross. (This is called propitiation in theological circles.) He then says to them "Follow me," and He will subsequently sanctify them along their journey. They will discover that God is not mad, but glad, as we see in Hebrews 1.9 *"Therefore, O God, your God has anointed you, pouring out the oil of joy (gladness) on you more than on anyone elsewhere."* Gladness is Jesus' chief characteristic as he receives the Spirit! That means there is no one in the universe with more joy than Jesus. It is covering Him from head to toe, just like the anointing oil on the priests of old (Ps. 133.2). When we embrace Jesus, that oil of gladness gets all over us. This is what I want to do: embrace Jesus and get that oil of gladness all over me, and then show others that He wants to embrace them too. Then that joy will spread over them and cause their hearts to open more and more. There is nothing more attractive than joy. Sounds like a good assignment, doesn't it?

STREET LEVEL PRAYER

28

Chapter 5

SEE WHAT GOD IS DOING

Back before Pam and I had our children, we used to ride our bicycles every weekend for fitness and recreation. We would ride on day tours with the local bicycle shop, the Steady Peddler and enjoy the (mostly) great weather of southern California. One weekend the shop sponsored a talk by the current world record holder for a trans-continental bicycle ride. I don't remember the time it took him, but it was an amazing feat of endurance and stamina. What I do remember is the answer he gave during the Q and A session when someone simply asked how he did it. He said, "I found someone who was doing what I wanted to do well, and I learned from him. What he did, I did, and what he didn't do, I didn't do. If you want to do something special, find someone who has already done it. It's pretty simple." That has always stuck with me. There is wisdom in those words, and it is Biblical wisdom.

Jesus said He only did what He saw the Father doing (Jn. 5.19). Once we get into prayer on the streets or marketplace, we want to observe what it is God is doing. There are several components to this, including visual information and revelation (both will be covered soon), as well as simply asking the person receiving prayer, "What is happening?" The reason for this is that we want to give individuals a way to put into words what they are experiencing during the prayer exchange. I usually say, "So, as I was praying for you, what was happening?" Their response can be anything from, "Oh, I felt peaceful" to something surprising like, "I really sensed God here with me" or even "I felt heat go through all of my body." This gives us an indication of what the Father is doing. I will try to get them to explain it in more detail by saying, "Tell me more." This will reveal the thing that God is putting His finger on, what God is doing, and that tells us what to do next. Usually it means an opening for more prayer: prayer for healing, prayer for salvation, or prayer for deliverance. This way we only do what God is doing, and we don't end up doing something that God is not doing. It's pretty simple, really.

The first question is purposefully open-ended, because we don't want to give an expectation or limit their response. We don't want to say "Did you feel anything?" because that limits the response to a feeling. We also want to avoid saying "What was God doing?" because some people won't be able to perceive it as "God." Some will say "It was nice" and that is all. No need to push them for more, because we trust that God is indeed at work and this is part of their journey toward Christ. I feel no pressure to "close the deal" in any prayer exchange because I know God is bringing His Kingdom as I love and pray for people. Some are ready for more, and we trust that they will tell us where they are in that journey. Some are ready to receive Christ as their Savior, and there will be evidence that they are at that point. Some of this is like fruit checking: some fruit is just ready to fall off the tree, and we just need to catch it. Other people need healing, and we are ready to pray for that as well. Others just need to be listened to and loved. This is all part of being available to God to help others experience the Kingdom of God, which is righteousness, peace and joy in the Holy Spirit (Rom. 14.17).

Doing only what the Father is doing is not as mystical as it may seem to some. It can be as simple as asking a person, who is created in His image, "What was happening as I was praying for you?" God can reveal His desire and His will through human responses. The key is to listen – really listen. Listen to the individual's story carefully, and we can often see where God is at work. Listen to the response to the follow-up question after the initial prayer, and we will discover more. God has given us the Holy Spirit to help us see what the Father is doing, and if we will observe and listen well, He will direct us. I like to call wisdom the "what to do next" gift. He will use our intellect, our experience, our training, and our gifting to show us the most important thing to do. We just try to see what the Father is doing in that moment, and cooperate with Him in His work. And if you love the people God sends you, you really can't go wrong.

Chapter 6

KEEP YOUR EYES OPEN

John Wimber, the founder of the Vineyard movement once said, "We came into the Vineyard worshiping with our eyes open and praying with our eyes closed. Now we have learned to worship with our eyes closed and pray with our eyes open." I was raised in the Lutheran church, which is where I met my wife, Pam. We were trained to pray with our eyes closed, and I still do that in my private time of prayer with the Lord (unless I'm driving!) But one of the keys to being effective in praying for people on the street or in the marketplace is learning to keep our eyes open in prayer. I mean this literally. (There is the concept of keeping the eyes of our heart open as well, Eph. 1.18.) Our eyes will be open as we learn to see what the Father is doing. This will seem strange for many at first, yet with practice you will become more comfortable with this way of praying.

I usually do it this way: Once I have listened to the person and have heard her story, I want to move into prayer. (Some will want to talk and talk, but never get into prayer). I start by saying "Let's pray right now" and I begin the prayer with initially bowing my head and closing my eyes. This tells the person that prayer has begun, but then in a moment I look up and open my eyes as I pray the prayer. Sometimes if the person is un-churched she will have her eyes open too, and she will be looking right at you! Don't let this distract you, as you can keep praying in a relational manner just the same. You are talking to God, yet you are speaking into the individual's heart and spirit. We are still praying, but our eyes are open and we are connecting with the Lord as we minister to the individual.

You do want to have your eyes open as you pray so that you are aware of the individual's response and the activity of the Holy Spirit. This helps you know what to do next, which is wisdom. This is one of the areas I comment on frequently when training novices out on the street doing prayer ministry. Out of habit, they close their eyes when it is their turn to pray at the booth. It may take a little practice to pray with eyes open, but it will come more naturally over time.

I want to see what God might be doing in the person and also see any clues given by body language or response. For example, if the person is shaking his head side to side (indicating "no") while I pray, I need to see that and respond. (If my eyes are closed, I will miss an important clue.) I will usually stop the prayer fairly quickly at that point and ask "What's wrong?" Remember, this is a relational and not religious activity, and we should feel free to talk to both the individual and to God. On the other hand, if he is nodding his head up and down (indicating "yes") there is a good chance that my prayers are hitting the spot. There is non-verbal communication going on, and our eyes need to be open to see it.

There are a myriad of physical responses that individuals may have during a prayer exchange, and we need to be observant. If we don't know what something means, we can always ask "What was happening as I was praying for you?" Some phenomena can be an indication of the work of the Holy Spirit in a person. Common ones include eye movement, eyelid flutter, tremors, shaking, increased breathing (rapid respiration), twitches, and losing the ability to stand (falling). We want to observe these things, and praying with our eyes open enables us to do that. We should, in most cases, keep praying when we see this happen, and allow God to do His work in them. When we finish praying, we can even ask them about what we observed, helping the person process what was going on in them.

Some phenomena might, but not always, indicate the presence of a demonic spirit. These may include eyes rolling back, facial grimacing, or the clinching of fists or teeth. I cannot cover deliverance ministry adequately here, but suffice it to say, God will give you what you need in the moment. I have done some deliverance on the street, but most has been with mild demonic attachment. You can only do what can be done in a short exchange. We will cover more on deliverance in a later chapter, but the observation of these clues is vital. If the individual is manifesting the presence of a demonic spirit physically, we need to be able to see that happening. Having our eyes closed in that situation would be foolish and potentially dangerous. I don't fear demons, but I do give them a healthy respect and proper caution.

Judging phenomena can be tricky, and we must be careful in assigning a cause to what we are observing. Some things that look strange and bizarre may actually be the work of the Holy Spirit, and if we automatically attribute that to demonic activity we are making a huge mistake. Likewise, some activity that looks "religious" could actually be demonic, and we will need to have discernment or the gift of distinguishing between spirits to recognize that. For example, I have seen people shake violently, to the point where I fear for their physical health and well-being, yet it is clear later that it was a response to the powerful work of the Holy Spirit being manifest in them. On the other hand, I have seen people "speak in other tongues" while being prayed for, yet it was not the Holy Spirit speaking, but a demonic utterance. God will give us the gifts we need at the point of need. He will show us the source of phenomenon if we will be patient and humble. The key here is not to jump to conclusions in our own understanding.

I don't want to give the impression that most of the people I pray for have physical manifestations. Some may be reading this and think, "If people start freaking out when I pray for them you need to find someone else to do this!" I would say only a small percentage of the individuals I pray for, maybe five percent, show some type of physical response in prayer that we would call "unusual." And the vast majority of that is a positive experience with the Holy Spirit. It is just good to be aware of what can happen in rare cases, and that knowledge will serve you well if and when you do come across it. It is my experience that God will give abundant grace when we take risks in faith and head into new territory. Anyone who says their Christianity is boring is probably doing it wrong!

Chapter 7

PROPHECY IN THE STREETS

One of the great blessings of my childhood was my relationship with my grandfather, Dr. Fred Staubach. As my mother was an only child, my brother, sister and I were his only grandchildren, and he spent plenty of time with us. He was an amazing man, and he lived to be 103 years old. As a child, I have very fond memories of him taking great interest in me. He would take time to talk with me about my life and showed genuine interest in the things that interested me. He was a life-long learner, and in addition to his two masters degrees and his doctorate, he was always taking classes. He spoke five languages and was even taking a Spanish class the year before he died!

Once, in a time of prayer, a memory of my grandfather stood out: God spoke to me in a prophetic picture based on a clear memory from my childhood. I was spending the night at his house, and being about eight years old at the time, I became frightened when I awoke alone in the dark. When I came into his room, I asked if it was all right if I got in bed with him. He consented, and so as I was falling asleep I remember being safe and warm. The thing I remember most was his smell – it was something like the combination of coffee, cologne and hair tonic. There was something very comforting about that smell, and it made me feel very safe. God brought that memory back to me all those years later and showed me that it was a prophetic image of how God cares for me. My grandfather was a type of my Heavenly Father who was comforting and keeping me safe. If God has a smell, and I think He does, it must be similar to the smell of Grandpa Staubach.

The major sign of the coming of the Kingdom of God at the advent of Jesus Christ is the restoration of the gift of prophecy. In other words, God has restored communication between Himself and His people because of the life, death, and resurrection of Jesus, who is the One anointed with the Holy Spirit (the Christ). At Pentecost, Peter declares that the sign of this new age of the Spirit is prophecy (Acts 2.17-18). And this gift is not just for a select group of God's people, such as prophets, judges and kings, but for all of His children. All those who know Jesus have the Holy Spirit, and all can hear the voice of God. It's for everyone, and the Lord is speaking all the time. We just need to learn how to listen.

An exciting aspect of doing street and marketplace ministry is seeing how God delights in giving us gifts of the Holy Spirit for this work. One of these is the gift of prophecy. It has been my experience that gifts are given at a point of need, and when we are really dependent on God to come through, He does! If you have been saying to God, "I really want to hear your voice. Please speak to me," then a good way to help facilitate that is to place yourself in a position where you need to hear from God for others. I like to use the passage in Psalm 139 that says *"How precious are your thoughts about me, O God. They cannot be numbered! I can't even count them; they outnumber the grains of sand!"* God has constant, precious thoughts towards us, and they are in the trillions! I think of that as a constant waterfall of wonderful, loving and affirming thoughts from God that are falling on me and everyone around me. When I am ministering to someone, I picture this prophetic waterfall coming down on them, and try to put myself under it so I can hear some of those precious thoughts. I only need one of the "grains of sand," so it's not like God is withholding that from me. To the contrary, He is more than willing to give us revelation that will open up the hearts of His children. We just need to ask.

Prophecy in the context of praying for people usually entails God giving us revelation about how He feels about that individual. This may also include information about them that we wouldn't have by natural means. It may come to us by impressions, pictures, words, or other means of revelation. This revelation must be weighed in our hearts and minds as we discern what God is saying (interpretation). In most settings of street ministry, God is often giving us information (revelation) that He wants us to share with others to bless them. The question then becomes: How do I deliver this prophecy to the individual in a way that is both relational and understandable?

I have struggled with this question for a while, and wanted to find a good balance between delivering a word (or that revelation from God) and not being weird or religious. Over time I have followed this technique to good success: Pray the "word" over the person and don't stop the prayer to give a "word." Saying it another way, I often receive revelation from God as I am praying for an individual, and I have learned to pray that as prophecy over them in the course of the prayer exchange. The key phrase I use is "Lord, I thank you that…" and then say the word in that prayer.

For example, if I get the picture of a father tossing a young child up and down in a playful way, I might say in midst of the prayer, "…and Lord, I thank you that you want to take Philip in your arms like a Father does a young boy and toss him in the air and catch him. You will always catch him. You love Philip and you smile and have joy as you two play together." I don't stop the prayer and say, "And the Lord would say to you, Philip…" because that would seem awkward and weird to most people (even most Christians) in that context. When the Lord gives me a scripture verse in prayer, I use the same phrase, "Lord, I thank you that…you have loved Philip with an everlasting love, you have drawn him with unfailing kindness" (Jer. 31.3). If the Lord is giving me information about Philip's past, I pray that in the middle of the prayer too, not stopping to give a "word of knowledge," but weaving it into the relational dialogue of the prayer exchange.

I always keep in mind the goal of loving people by being relational as possible, and by removing any barriers that would keep them from receiving what God wants to give. Could prophecy be delivered in an un-loving way? Sure, and I have been the recipient of someone's attempt to prophesy over me in a harsh, forceful manner that did not communicate God's love. If there was true revelation in there, it got lost in the manner of delivery. I want to avoid doing that at all cost, so I try to put myself in the shoes of the person receiving prayer and prophecy. I want to get out of the way of God, and not make the ministry about me. The more powerful and gifted you are in ministry, the more you have to commit to not making yourself the center of attention. Prophecy always should have Jesus as the focus, and it should have the aroma (smell) of the Son of God on it. *"For the essence of prophecy is to give a clear witness for Jesus"* (Rev. 19.10 NLT). The gift of prophecy in the context of street prayer serves to open up the heart of the individual to the love and power of God (1Cor. 14.25). It is very wonderful when that happens, and God is delighted to speak through us.

Chapter 8

ONE THING AT A TIME

In the gospels we find an interesting story of the sisters, Martha and Mary. This story is often used as a contrast between service and devotion, and rightly so. But if you look deeper, you may see an underlying truth about the "one thing" that Mary chose for which she was commended. To put it simply, this one thing is to be with Jesus: to rest with Him and listen to His words. It seems Jesus has a single focus on His agenda: for us to be in His presence and listen. *"Martha, Martha," the Lord answered, "You are worried and upset about many things, but few things are needed—or indeed only one. Mary has chosen what is better, and it will not be taken away from her"* (Lk. 10.41-42). To bring this forward into the context of street ministry, I have realized that my agenda needs to be the same: to be with Jesus and listen! It's easy to get concerned for the many things that "need to be done" in the individual's life as I listen to his or her story. But Jesus' agenda is more concise; and He wants to be present with us and speak to one area of need.

Over the course of praying for thousands of people on the street and in the marketplace, I have come to understand that God usually has one thing He wants to do with an individual in that short prayer exchange. He wants to be present and make Himself known as He touches one specific area of a life. I'm trying to be present with Jesus in that moment, and as I listen, both to the Lord and to the person (we call this "L-Shaped" listening, as it is vertical and horizontal), I will help the person become present with Jesus as well. It is in that moment that Jesus will speak to him or her in some way that only He can, meeting that one need.

I usually tell people before, during, or after the prayer that God had an appointment with them on His calendar, and even though they didn't know about it, I was just helping them keep it. This is not just a nice thing to say; it is actually true! This encounter at the booth is not happenstance or luck or fortune or a random chance encounter. This is a divine appointment that was planned before the foundation of the earth. As we talk and pray with these individuals, we begin to understand God's objective for this exchange. For some, it is to encounter the love of God because someone is willing to listen to them and take the time to pray for them. For others, it is the time to receive healing from God, whether it is physical, emotional, or spiritual. Some individuals need the edification, strengthening or comfort that comes in a prophetic prayer exchange. And some are ready to experience new life in Christ for the first time, as this is their salvation moment.

The key to this is the understanding that you can't do everything in one exchange, but only need to do one thing. This brings tremendous freedom for us who are praying and ministering in the street and marketplace. The pressure is off to make anything and everything happen. We discover what God's one agenda item is in this prayer exchange by being good listeners: listening to people and listening to God. As we are receiving information from people (verbal and non-verbal) and information from God (revelation), it is good to ask some questions. After the basic one, "So, as I was praying for you, what was happening?" I might ask them to give me more details about what is really occurring in their life. At the same time I am listening to God for revelation of what He wants to do for that person. In my spirit I might be praying something like this as I'm listening to a woman named Rebecca: "Lord Jesus, You are present here with us. Make Yourself known to Rebecca, and show me what to do next." This is really a silent prayer for wisdom, or as I call it, the "what to do next" gift.

Often, as a matter of course, I will ask people if they have any health issues or concerns, and then move into prayer for healing. Others will want prayer about relational issues, and this often leads to prayer for emotional healing. All of this is based on what we can discern during our encounter about God's agenda for that moment. I always try to do this in a relational and conversational way. I don't push people, and I don't try to take them somewhere they don't want to go. They must come freely, and as the Holy Spirit gets involved, people will usually tell you what they need. We bring Jesus into the conversation by being loving and affirming. Jesus will be present, and He will do what only He can do. When that has been done, we have completed our assignment with the knowledge that we have done everything we were supposed to do, and nothing more. That brings a peace that passes all understanding (Phil. 4.7).

Chapter 9

HANDS-OFF PRAYING

Have you ever been picked out of an audience to participate in some kind of show or performance? For some reason, I always seem to be that guy who performers pick out of the crowd to come up on stage. In fact, it has happened so many times that I will literally hide behind others when it gets to that point in a performance. One time, at a renaissance festival, two jugglers picked me out of an audience to stand between them as they passed large machetes back and forth. They were making jokes about my safety as these blades were spinning inches from my face! This was not a pleasant experience to be the center of attention and the focus of others' derision. I think most of the others in the audience were thinking, "I'm sure glad they didn't pick me. Poor guy!" Now you know why I hide!

One of the common questions I get asked about prayer ministry in the street and marketplace is: "Should I lay hands on people when I pray for them?" My general answer, which might surprise some of you, is "no" (regardless of what the cover of the book might show!). For those of us who have a charismatic or Pentecostal background, it would seem almost blasphemous not to put our hands on people as we pray for them! But my reasoning is based on the principle that loving people is paramount, and we want to avoid doing anything that will make them feel uncomfortable in a public prayer exchange. Prayer, whether it is on the street corner or in the Farmers' Market, is a visible public interchange. The individual receiving prayer is aware that others might be looking on, and there is already a level of discomfort as we begin to pray. We need to be able to put ourselves in the person's shoes, and try to feel what she is feeling. Putting our hands on someone will, in most cases, add to her feeling of being an "object" of attention, and will detract from her ability to relax and receive what God is doing in the moment. Loving the person is putting her feelings and response ahead of our agenda to do a "spiritual" practice.

So if we don't lay hands on people, are they missing something from God? I don't think so, because God seems to be able to do what He desires without it. Without going into a Biblical teaching on the practice of laying on of hands, I would summarize the topic by saying it is connected with healing, empowerment, and ordination in the scriptures, but not in every case. There are many texts, especially describing healing and empowerment, where there is no mention of the practice of laying on of hands. (And I have yet to have an opportunity to do ordination on the streets!) I have seen many people healed or empowered where I have not touched them in any way. It is the presence of Jesus that is required, and He is able to touch people by His Spirit just fine without me making any physical contact.

What about holding hands while praying? Again, it is dependent on the context and the environment, but I usually only hold hands if the person being prayed for initiates it. Even then we must use discernment. I have witnessed one case where a team was trying to minister deliverance to an individual who wanted to hold hands. As soon as the prayer started, he clamped down hard and wouldn't let go! Granted, this is an extreme example, yet we must use wisdom. I try to practice the type of ministry where my prayers are just an extension of the conversation I am having with the individual. If I am talking with people on the street, I generally don't hold hands with them or put my palm on their forehead! I want the prayer exchange to be just as relational and conversational as talking. The only difference is we are talking and listening to God as well.

On some occasions I have felt prompted by the Lord to ask

permission to lay hands on individuals during prayer, but it seems to be the exception rather than the rule. (I once had a guy ask me to hit him on the head when I prayed for his healing!) Of course wisdom and common sense should tell us to be very careful about men putting their hands on women and vice versa. If I do lay hands on people in this setting, it is usually lightly on the shoulder. But for the most part, I recommend just praying with your eyes open like you are still talking to the person, with your hands at your side and your heart open to God. Focus on the individual in front of youthat He loves. God will do the touching!

Chapter 10

DON'T TRY TO "CLOSE THE DEAL"

I think everyone has had a least one terrible job in their lives, and for many it comes when we are young and just starting out in the work world. For me it was when I was in my sophomore year of college and I took a job selling vacuum cleaners! It was commission-only pay, and to make any money you had to "close the deal" and make a sale. What a horrible job that was, as I had to go into the home of strangers and convince them that their house was filthy and they needed to buy a very expensive vacuum to clean it up. I was not very good at it, as I only closed four deals in about three months. It was remarkable to me how anyone could make a living doing that. I have empathy and respect for people whose livelihood is tied to sales. (Now this time was not wasted, as God used this experience many years later to prepare me for home and hospital visitations of the sick and dying; but that's a story for another time.)

There is a sense in which we can also have the mentality of "closing the deal" when we are involved in street ministry. "What if I pray for someone and nothing happens?" I hear this from people all the time as I teach on healing and street prayer ministry. I understand the question, and I have asked it myself, but I have found that it is based on some faulty presuppositions. The first is that somehow it is up to me to make something happen in prayer.

The reality is that I cannot make anything "happen," as this is God's realm and He is both the initiator of prayer and the One who answers. It's a mystery, this thing we do called prayer, but the truth is God is the beginning and end of it; we just play some role in the middle of it all and in His grace He chooses to include us in it.

The second false idea is that "nothing" happening is a real possibility in prayer, even when God is involved. I feel that both of these presuppositions are based on an inadequate view of the Kingdom of God. It is my understanding that Jesus is indeed King, and that when I call upon the name of the Lord it is up to Him to "make something happen." The pressure is off me because I can't do anything of value or with a spiritual outcome without God anyway (Jn. 15.5). I operate in ministry on the street or marketplace with the mindset that God loves me and loves the people for whom I am praying. He sent me to do this, and it is part of His master plan of disciple making. Therefore, He will always bring His Kingdom when I pray, and there is never a time when the Kingdom of God does not come in some real way.

Now the Kingdom of God might not come in the way I was thinking or hoping, but God will always bring the Kingdom of righteousness, peace and joy in the Holy Spirit (Rom. 14.17). This verse is helpful if we unpack it to see what God might be doing in any given prayer exchange where the Kingdom comes. It has been my experience that one or more of these Kingdom components is present whenever we pray for others. Righteousness is relational justice, being made right with God and in turn, right with others. Peace is the presence of God bringing wholeness, including physical wellness and relational unity. Joy is an awareness of God's grace and favor, including a superabundance of the gladness of God. These are all really good things for people to experience, and it would be incorrect to equate these expressions of the Kingdom's presence with "nothing happening." Sometimes the Kingdom's presence is occurring on the inside of the individual, and we need to ask questions to help them express what is happening internally.

When I have this perspective on the Kingdom of God breaking in on every prayer exchange, it frees me up from trying to "close the deal" with people. That is the Spirit's job, and I cannot do His job. My job is to be available to God (show up), love people the best I can, and invite them to receive a blessing as I pray the love of God over them. He brings the Kingdom when we invite Him to, and He often does more than we could ask or think (Eph. 3.20). Only God can touch a soul, heal a body, or set a mind free. Only God can put His finger on what is really wrong and make it right. And only God can bring His perspective on what seems to be a difficult, desperate or impossible situation.

It would be extreme pride to think I could do any of that myself. But I have seen God do these things hundreds of times. In addition, we should not prod, push, or pressure people to do something to make "it" happen either. But if we invite people to receive a touch from God, He will touch them. And as we pray that His Kingdom come, and His will be done, on earth as it is in heaven, there is a divine exchange between heaven and earth. "Something" always happens, and it is always good (2Chron. 7.3).

Chapter 11

PRAYING FOR HEALING ON THE STREETS

On March 18th, 1993 my life drastically changed. I was playing basketball with some students at the school where I was a teacher. I came down with a rebound and turned to outlet a pass, when my back locked up! I was in severe pain; later I was diagnosed with two herniated lumbar discs. My life up to that point was focused around sports and athletics. I was teaching physical education, playing tennis, racquetball and basketball regularly, riding my bicycle, and coaching and officiating basketball. That all ended in that moment of injury. I became stuck in a cycle of pain and no matter what I did, that pain didn't leave.

Where was God? I didn't have an answer, yet it became clear that my life would never go back to what it was. I needed healing, and I believed in healing, yet I was not being healed. This took me on a journey of learning about pain, and discovering God's heart for those who suffer. Over time I have received a good measure of healing in my back, yet the course of my life was forever altered. And for me, that course was sovereignly altered by God for my good, and the good of others. Why didn't God heal me right away and take away my pain the first day I received prayer for healing? It's a complicated question, but in the final analysis I have come to understand that God is good, and He knows what He is doing. Each of our situations is unique, and God is working in us His good will and pleasure. One of the interesting things that has happened in my ministry is I seem to have very good success in seeing results when I pray for healing for others' back pain! It's a mystery, yet I keep pressing into the healing ministry of Jesus.

Recently, I have seen more physical healing outside the walls of the church than I have inside the church. So much more, in fact, that I don't think it is an exaggeration to say I have seen more healing on the streets and in the marketplace in the last seven years than I have seen in the last 25 years of my ministry inside the church. I am not clear on all the reasons for this, and there may be many, but one seems to be that God loves to show up and let people know He is real outside the church. And one of the ways He does this is by healing their bodies! Some people talk about being at the right place at the right time, and yet if we make ourselves available to God to pray for healing wherever we go, we seem to be in the right place all the time.

So how do we go about doing healing on the streets and in the marketplace? To begin with, we need to position ourselves to offer healing to people in a way that conveys love and acceptance. And we want to provide this ministry in a way that seems naturally-supernatural and not weird. No hype, no drama, just real people asking God to do what only God can do. In many cases, but not all, there is substantial healing that is measurable and remarkable. In the situation where there is no remarkable result, I believe that the Kingdom of God has indeed come, as people are cared for and loved. We just don't have all the information to evaluate it properly from God's perspective.

Most prayer for healing on the streets begins with me asking a question after an initial prayer exchange, "Do you have any health concerns at this time? Any medical problems? Any pain?" If they do (and most people have something physically wrong), I will offer to pray for healing. Because they have already received prayer from me, they usually say "OK," and I begin by asking the Lord to come with His healing. From that point it is not so much "prayer" but more of "doing healing." With the exception of James 5, we see most of the healing ministry in the New Testament as "doing healing" and not "prayer" for healing. Because we have a short time, I usually go right into a command and tell whatever is wrong to be made right. I do this in a normal voice and volume, and I just talk to the body and tell it to function properly.

If Tim has pain in the right knee because of cartilage loss, I will ask him his pain level from 1 to 10 before I pray. Then I might pray something like, "Lord Jesus, thank you that you love Tim. I ask you to bring your Kingdom and gifts of healings by the Holy Spirit. Right now I tell the right knee to function properly and all structures to be made whole and come under the obedience of Christ. I tell all pain to leave the body, in Jesus' Name." Then I will ask Tim to move the knee and say "OK, what is your pain level now?" I might even say, "Is it better, the same, or worse?" I want people to be free to tell me the truth about how it feels so we can see if any healing is happening. If healing has happened there will be evidence. For some, this is the moment of truth, both as the pray'er and the pray'ee. If the pain level goes down, but is still lingering, I will ask to pray again, usually up to three or four times, depending on the context.

We want to deal with the reality of what God is doing, and thank Him for whatever is happening. We don't pretend healing is there when there is no evidence, and we don't want to minimize any healing that has happened as well. When I first started out praying for healing I wouldn't ask how people were doing afterward because I didn't really want to know. If they were not healed I would be embarrassed. Now that my practice and theology of healing has changed, I try to get feedback whenever possible. I always invite people for more prayer in the future if healing is incomplete, and ask them to come back and let us know when healing happens progressively or at a later time. If they are healed substantially, I encourage them to tell someone else what God has done.

There is a famous story told about John Wimber, the founder of the Vineyard Church, in regard to the practice of praying for healing. Someone came to him and said, "I tried that healing prayer thing with someone and it didn't work." Wimber replied, "Go pray for a hundred people and then come talk to me." There is a reason that they call the medical profession a "practice." The same can be said for the healing ministry, and the more we do it, the more results we will begin to see. It's more than just a numbers game too, as we will learn from each prayer encounter to become better listeners and better practitioners of Jesus' healing ministry. When I started out, I was always surprised when someone was healed. Now it seems I'm more surprised when they aren't. But we have to start somewhere, and we can't get discouraged when things don't seem to be going well. In the case of healing, practice doesn't make perfect, but practice does make better. I can't think of many things more worth our time than participating in the healing ministry of Jesus.

Chapter 12

LEADING SOMEONE TO CHRIST

The way I have summarized my salvation experience is as follows: I spent the first 20 years of my life running from Jesus. He got tired of chasing me and tackled me from behind. Then I turned around and said, "Jesus, I found you!" That may not be completely accurate theologically, but in a general sense it's true. I was raised in a Christian home, and both of my older siblings came to know Christ through the tail end of the Jesus People Movement (back in the 60s and 70s when Jesus moved to California!). I was the proverbial black sheep of the family, and wanted nothing to do with God in my teen years. What I didn't know at the time was that my mom was a closet prayer warrior! She was interceding for me on a regular basis, asking God to save me from the path I was on. Those bowls of prayer that were stored in heaven started to get poured out my sophomore year of college.

I was on campus when I bumped into an old acquaintance from the Lutheran church I had attended growing up. Bill Urich and I had gone through confirmation classes together at St. Luke's, but I had not seen him since junior high school. He said to me, "Hey Todd, I haven't seen you at church in years. You must really be backslidden!" He probably meant it as a joke, but God pierced my heart with that comment. I started to panic, and figured that God was on campus, so I went to my car to get away from God. But God was in my car too, so I didn't get far. About two blocks from the school I had to pull over to the side of the road because I couldn't see through the tears. In that holy and divine moment I prayed and surrendered my life to Jesus. No more running from God. It was finally time to start following Him instead.

While I don't recommend calling people "backsliders" as a means of evangelism, it is a great blessing and privilege to be the person that the Spirit uses to help bring someone to the point of receiving Christ. When we are ministering on the street or marketplace, we often get the opportunity to meet people who are very near the place of salvation. For many Christians, the word "evangelism" brings anxiety, and for others it brings guilt. I really don't view what I do to lead people to the Lord as evangelism, per se, because all of them are at a point in their life where they are ready. I'm not using a method to witness or get a "conversion." What I do is find out where people are in their journey toward Christ. Those that are already at a point of recognizing their need to receive Him, I help midwife into the Kingdom. Another analogy I like to use is fruit checking. When the fruit is ready for harvest, it is just a matter of catching it as it falls off the tree. There is never any arguing or apologetics at this point – just new life being birthed. And when you get to be a part of that once it makes you hungry for more.

One of the great things about doing a "Need Prayer?" Booth is that many of the people who come for prayer are in crisis and they are open to God in ways they weren't before. As I pray for them and ask them questions, I get a feel for where they are spiritually. A good, non-threatening question I like to ask is, "Where do you feel you are in your journey with God?" I find this much more preferable to questions like, "Are you saved?" or "Have you found Jesus yet?" Those questions tend to put people on the defensive, and I want them to be open to God. Even an atheist can say, "I don't have a journey with God because I don't believe He exists." Most people can describe their journey without feeling threatened or put on the spot. This answer will tell you what to do next. At this point if they seem "close," the Holy Spirit will often prompt me to ask them about their relationship to Christ. I don't do this with everyone that comes for prayer, but only those who seem "ready." Their answers will show you that they are looking for God, or they are interested in knowing more about Him. This is where it gets exciting!

I will ask this person, "Has there ever been a time in your life when you received Jesus Christ as your savior?" I use this phrase because it is to the point and can usually be answered in a yes/no response. I use the term "received" because I think it conveys the idea of the response of the individual to the prompting or offer from God of salvation (Jn. 1.12, Col. 2.6). If they say "yes," I ask them to tell me about it. Sometimes the story is not a Biblical salvation story, but something like, "I went to church when I was a child." But in most cases they answer "no," and I then say something like, "Based on what you told me about your situation, I think that this would be a good place to start. I can help you pray to receive Jesus Christ as your savior – would you like to do that?" Surprisingly, if I have read the situation right, most people say "yes!"

Then I lead them in a prayer of the A.B.C.'S. (This is just a way for me to remember what to include and is not intended to be a formula). I will ask them to repeat after me (each sentence) a prayer something like this: "Dear Jesus, thank You that You love me. I admit I have made lots of mistakes and bad decisions in my life (A=Admit your sin). I have sinned against You, against others and against myself. I believe You died on the cross for my sins and rose from the dead to give me life (B=Believe in Jesus). I commit my life to You, Jesus, and ask you to forgive me for trying to live my life without You (C=Commit my life). I receive all that You have done for me and ask You to fill me with the Holy Spirit right now (S=Spirit filling). Thank You for saving me now, in Jesus' name, amen."

This prayer can take many forms, and you can add or replace some of the elements of the prayer, as God looks on the heart of the individual. The key is to help the person respond and receive what the Holy Spirit is doing to bring them to Jesus. I try to keep the sentences short, just like a minister leading a bride and groom in their vows. I pray this same prayer for those who want to re-commit their lives to Christ. Many come to us for prayer and then as the Holy Spirit is at work in that space, they will want to repent and come back to following Jesus. Only God can know what's in someone's heart, and only He knows who is saved and who belongs to Him. I don't get caught up in trying to decide who's in and who is out. I'm just one hungry beggar showing others where I found food.

The follow-up then focuses on helping them find a Christian community where they can grow and develop. Again, we can't do everything, but we can help point them in the right direction. If they are near your local church, by all means invite them to come. If they live elsewhere refer them to another congregation. We can offer suggestions, but we should not become co-dependent with people, taking responsibility for their continued journey toward Christ. That is the Holy Spirit's job, and we have to get to a point where we trust that He will continue this work. I'm just thankful that I am allowed to play some role in this wonderful story of salvation history.

Chapter 13

WHAT ABOUT DELIVERANCE?

It was about 2 a.m. and I was sound asleep when the phone rang. It was my senior pastor calling to say there was a demonized man he was bringing to the church and he wanted me to help with the deliverance. This was about twenty five years ago, and I didn't know any better, so I said I'd meet him there as soon as I could. (Now I would tell them to wait until morning!) I lived close to the church, so I was the first to arrive. I had never really done deliverance before, so in the extra time I got out my Bible and found the place in Luke's gospel where it says of Jesus that He gave His followers "power and authority to drive out all demons." I was not sure what to expect, but I did know that I was a Jesus follower, so He had given me authority too. I just wasn't sure how to use it.

When we all went into the church office I was relieved. Not only was the pastor there, but so was the pastoral counselor, so I figured I was going to be in a supporting role. And the so-called demonized guy looked pretty normal to me. He wasn't foaming at the mouth and his head wasn't spinning around, so I concluded I would be safe and let the professional Christians handle this. I would just watch and pray. We sat in a circle, with the pastor and the counselor sitting next to the man on each side, while I was across from him. Someone had the brilliant idea of holding hands, so I held hands with the two professionals while they held hands with the man. The second we started to pray the man's face changed and he clamped down hard on the two hands he was holding! The pastor was able to force his hand out using his other hand as a tool, but the counselor couldn't get his hand out, not matter how hard he pulled.

At that moment a boldness and authority came on me. I can only describe it as a supernatural confidence in the situation that I didn't have the minute prior. I found myself taking over the situation and saying to the man, "Stop that right now! Let go of his hand and look at me." He let go of the counselor's hand. Just prior to this the man had started to talk in a strange voice and was spewing out profanity. Again, I spoke with a confidence, "Be silent." He stopped talking. I continued, "I tell any demonic spirit to leave him right now in the name of Jesus Christ." The man slumped in his chair like he had been shot. Both the pastor and the counselor looked at me and had expressions that said, "What just happened?" It was very fast and only lasted about a minute. For some reason God decided in that one moment to give me the authority to do what needed to be done. I really didn't know what I was doing, and yet the Lord showed up and took care of business. To this day I wonder why he picked me instead of the professionals. Now in my experience, this is not a typical deliverance session in many ways, but it was my introduction to it. I think God was showing me that He can handle any situation that may arise in Kingdom ministry.

As C.S. Lewis once said, there are two mistakes people make about the devil: One is to ignore or to deny his existence, and the other is to become too interested in him. When we do ministry on the street or in the marketplace, we will occasionally come across demonic activity in people. The question then becomes how to handle it in a healthy and sane way without falling into one of the above traps (ignoring or fixating). In this short chapter there is no way to deal with this topic in a comprehensive way, but some basic principles can be shared that should be of help.

Jesus has given us (the Church) authority over demonic spirits (in people), and we need not be afraid of them (Lk. 10. 17-19). Casting out demons is part of the demonstration of the Kingdom of

God, by Jesus and his followers (Lk. 9. 1-2). The term "demon possessed," as used in the KJV, is also problematic. The New Testament only has one word to describe all demonic activity, *daimonidzein.* (The Greek word *daimonidzein* means "to have a demon"). Possession (or total control) is an inaccurate concept. A better descriptive is "demonization." It is best to view demonic activity on a continuum, or degrees of demonic attachment on a scale from mild to moderate to strong. (Strong demonization would be like the Gadarene demoniac in Mark 5.) This is based on the amount of influence and control the demon(s) seem to have over the individual.

In the street or marketplace setting, the context and time constraint dictate that we usually only deal directly with mild demonic attachment in people that come for prayer. The reason for this is that stronger attachment is usually based on deep seated issues that need time and the proper setting to uncover. We need to guard against embarrassing people in public, and help them maintain their dignity. The individual is never the enemy, so we must treat the person with love and respect, even if they are demonized. People can be referred to ministries where they can receive this type of help, but in most cases it is unwise to try and do deliverance on the street. But others with milder attachment can be set free, and it is not uncommon for us to do this type of deliverance in a short prayer session.

Once you determine the presence of a demonic spirit, it is important to discern the basis for its presence. It has a legal right to be there, usually based on some type of sin or disobedience. The process we take them through is this: confession (what sin was committed), repentance (turning away from the sin, lie, or disobedience and turning toward God), and renouncing (taking any authority away from the demon(s), and rejecting their power). This may take the form of unrepentant sin, unforgiveness toward another, or some occult practice. The key is the Holy Spirit revealing the area of attachment, and then bringing His light into the situation. Asking questions is very helpful in this situation, as it can be a major problem if we make assumptions. It is not unusual to determine the presence of a demon in the course of a prayer session. I will say to the individual something like, "There seems to be an evil presence here. Do you sense that too? What do think has given it the legal right to be here?" In many cases the individual will not only sense this demon, but will know exactly why it is there. I will ask, "Do you want to get rid of it?" This may seem like a silly question, but there are times when people have made "friends" with "familiar" spirits, and they want to keep the power that that demon seems to give them. Of course they are deceived, but the individual must exercise their own will and choose to be free. If not, you are wasting your time.

If the individual wants to be free, I will lead them through the process of confession, repentance and renouncing. The person will be doing most of the work in this prayer (as they are led by the pray'er), and we must rely on the Holy Spirit to give them revelation. We do all this in a calm voice and with a loving and respectful attitude toward the individual. Love is the most powerful force in creation, and it is the perfect love of God that drives out fear (1Jn. 4.18). Remember that you only have a short time, so you can only do what you can do. If more needs to be done (and it probably will), they can be referred to a church or ministry for a follow up.

Some of you who are reading this might be thinking, "I don't want to have anything to do with this area. This is not for me." I totally understand that, yet if we are going to do Kingdom ministry, we will at times come across demonic activity in people. Setting people free from demons is part of the healing ministry of Jesus. In effect, this is part of the job description of being a Jesus follower. If we are His disciples, then we are apprentices who do what He did. We don't go looking for demons in every situation, but we do have authority to deal with them when they raise their ugly heads. The Kingdom call is to set captives free. Deliverance is part of that call.

Chapter 14

DEALING WITH THE RELIGIOUS SPIRIT

Most of you have met this person. There are many out there. They come across as the opinionated, unloving and inflexible religious nut. They give Christianity a bad name, and you find yourself avoiding them whenever possible whether it's at church, on your job or in your neighborhood. You may have started out in a relationship with them, thinking you had found kinship with another believer. But you quickly discovered that they have "another spirit."(2Cor. 11.14) These people are not spiritually attractive, but repulsive to everyone, believer and non-believer alike. You may have even tried to help them, by patiently pointing out the error of their theology or actions. But you have also quickly discovered that they won't listen. They will argue and debate, but no change ever occurs. They even seem to enjoy the fact that no one will agree with them, as it reinforces their cause by making them a martyr. They just become more entrenched in their position, and they are affirmed in their belief that they are one of the few right-thinking "remnant." Whether you knew it or not at the time, you most likely had come face to face with a "religious spirit."

If we pray and minister to people on the street or marketplace for any length of time, we will come across this "religious spirit." This is a term I use to describe an attitude in people who are intent on arguing about doctrine, and they tend to be very sectarian when it comes to churches and religious groups. You can recognize this fairly quickly when people don't want you to pray for them, but want to engage you in a heated discussion about points of theology and practice. They will try to draw you into debates about points of doctrine, and seem to always have pet proof texts on which they want your agreement. For some, this is just pride and spiritual immaturity, while with others this "spirit" is actually a demonic presence. They will often have Bible verses at the ready, and use plenty of Christian lingo, but make no mistake about it; these folks are divisive! Their "spirit" and argumentative interaction with you creates a spiritual repulsion to others who may be nearby. No positive ministry can take place while you are interacting with these individuals. You are almost always in a no-win situation.

I have found it best to disengage as quickly as possible. If I am at the "Need Prayer?" Booth I will say something like, "Well, I am here to pray for people, and not to argue, so I think it would be best if you leave now." If it is not my "turf," I will say goodbye and just walk away. This may seem harsh to some, but there has never in my experience been a good outcome in having a theological debate with this type of individual. Titus 3.9-11 warns us that these arguments are unprofitable and useless, and after warning such a person, we should have nothing to do with him or her.

In many cases, this type of person has been unwillingly or unknowingly used by the enemy to disrupt and hinder effective Kingdom ministry. Thankfully, such encounters are rare at the Prayer Booth. I can count on two hands the number of times I have had to ask someone to leave. Those who have a developed gift of the distinguishing of spirits can spot them a mile away. In fact, it is a good practice to pray at the beginning of a ministry outreach that God would keep away anyone who would disrupt His work that day.

Two other cautions are needed here. There is a danger of engaging with this type of individual because of our pride. We may think we know more about God and the Bible than they do, so we want to show them the error of their thinking. It almost never works! Even if you win the argument you will lose the battle. Or we could have misplaced compassion and think we can help change them. They are not looking for help or change. They are usually seeking out someone who will engage in an extended intellectual tug-of-war to reaffirm them in their delusion. Those with a "religious spirit" may seem rational and even highly spiritual, yet their presence in a ministry setting will create chaos. Experience has shown that it is best to separate from them quickly so that you will be free to minister the love and power of Jesus to those who really want it.

Chapter 15

TEAM MINISTRY AND MULTIPLICATION

I have been very blessed to have had some wonderful mentors in my life. In fact, for most of my Christian life I have sought them out. After observing men who were mature in their faith and godly in their character, I would approach them about being my mentor for a season. I could not imagine my life and ministry without the friendship and coaching of these men. The pinnacle of my mentors was Dr. Bill Jackson (Jax). You can read more about him in the Appendix, but for now let me just say that Jax had a very profound impact on my life and ministry.

One event in our relationship stands out as an example of his commitment to team ministry and discipleship. I was traveling with him at the time, watching him teach at conferences and seminars, and on this occasion we were in Omaha, Nebraska. He was teaching a seminar on "How to Minister Like Jesus." I had seen him teach this several times, but was not really prepared for what he did next. During the lunch break he told me he wanted me to teach the next section on the 5-step prayer model. I guess he thought I was ready, but I wasn't so sure. But he believed in me, so I got up and did my best. It seemed to go well, and afterward at the motel he said I did a great job. That was the beginning of our partnership in ministry that included not only seminars, but starting a Bible college as well. He wanted to give away what he had learned from the Lord, and I got to be the recipient of that great blessing.

I've seen one dynamic of mentoring and discipling change somewhat in the last few generations. It seems to me young men and women are not seeking mentors as a matter of course – they are waiting for mentors to come to them! The reason for this phenomenon is not clear to me fully, but it does change the way mentoring and coaching is initiated. If we are more mature in our faith and ministry, it is up to us to pray and seek God for the next generation of ministers and leaders. The chain will remain unbroken if we are open and willing to become mentors.

"And the things you have heard me say in the presence of many witnesses entrust to reliable people who will also be qualified to teach others" (2Tim. 2.2). There are four generations mentioned in this verse. The sequence is: Paul, then Timothy, then "reliable people," then "others." This truth came home to me in a special way when I was in seminary, taking a Hermeneutics class from Dr. Jackson. He said, "I'm teaching you the way I learned this from Dr. Gordon Fee. You will in turn teach this to others." I had a God moment in class right then, as I realized that what Paul said to Timothy was literally happening to me. Dr. Fee, then Jax, then me, then others I would teach would carry on the work. The chain of the "good deposit" (2Tim. 1.14) from God will continue as we pass it on.

Sometimes we seek out our "Timothy" and sometimes he seeks us out. I was doing my weekly Friday "Need Prayer?" Booth in Riverside when a middle-aged African-American couple stopped in for prayer. They told me they were pastoring a small Pentecostal church in nearby Moreno Valley, and were very excited to see how I was doing prayer outreach and wanted me to help them learn how to do one in their city. His name was Kerry Davis and his wife was Maria. I meet so many different people that say the same thing, but few ever follow up. Kerry talked me into giving him my cell number, but I quickly forgot about it. Then he called me the next day and left a message. I was busy with other things and didn't return his call. And then he called again a few days later and then again the next week. I started to think to myself, "This guy is persistent and seems to be serious about me helping him start a prayer booth in Moreno Valley." I'm not sure why I put him off for that number of calls, but it may have been due to the fact that we were from very different theological and social-racial backgrounds. I wasn't sure what I was doing would translate into his very different sphere of influence, but that was my bias and weakness showing through. I told him we could meet for lunch at a local restaurant and talk.

What happened at that meeting was that God simply showed me that even though Kerry and I were very different in many ways, we had the very same heart to reach people out on the street with the love of Jesus. He agreed to read over the material I gave him that day about doing outreach, and we planned to get together to start a prayer booth near his home. Not only did he read the material, but he and Maria had devoured it! They had notes in the margins and questions to ask. They were "all in" from the beginning. This began a wonderful relationship with Kerry and me, as we prayed for many individuals together every Thursday in Moreno Valley. (He also did the same location on Tuesday with Maria).

God gave him favor in that location (a supermarket and strip mall corner) with the owner and property manager. The area was known for gang activity and drug distribution, so the management gave him "unofficial" permission to set up the "Need Prayer?" Booth in a prime location. They were smart enough to understand that bringing God into the market might be a good thing for business! It was spiritual light in a very dark place, but the light of Christ will always prevail. Space does not permit a full telling of the story, but many healings and salvations have now occurred on that spot where there seems to be an "open heaven."

"Two are better than one, because they have a good return for their labor… Though one may be overpowered, two can defend themselves. A cord of three strands is not quickly broken" (Ecc. 4.9,12). Team ministry is always preferred to trying to go it alone. When I first started out doing the "Need Prayer?" Booth, I was, for the most part, on my own. Plenty of people told me they thought it was a great idea for outreach, but very few would join me, at least at the beginning. God was faithful, and I did see many people touched by God with healing and salvation, but I found that doing it as a team with others had many benefits. Jesus sent His disciples

out "two by two" (Lk. 10.1), and He seemed to know what He was doing! This doesn't mean we should never do ministry alone, but whenever possible, it is best to go as a team. There are many reasons for this, including discipleship, spiritual protection and multiplicity of gifts.

One major benefit of working as a team is the discipleship model we employ (Mat. 28.19, 20). It goes something like this: I do the ministry activity and you observe. Then we do this ministry together. Then you do ministry and I observe. Then you do ministry with someone new and give away what you have learned. Following each of these ministry exchanges we debrief. The debriefing time is essential as we talk about what occurred and evaluate. It is good to ask open-ended questions so that our partner engages in the discussion. "What did you notice?" "What did you see happening at this point?" "What do you think God was doing when this happened?" We, as mentors and coaches, are not providing all the answers here, but helping our partner discover and apply the wisdom and insights that the Holy Spirit supplies. We multiply discipleship and giftedness as we train and release others into ministry with this hands-on training. The only real way to learn and develop a new skill is by actually doing it.

When new ministry partners come to the "Need Prayer?" Booth for the first time, I usually have them observe me a few times as I pray for individuals, but I want them to get an experience with a prayer exchange right away. I brief them about the mandate of loving the people God will send us, and then ask them to participate in the prayer after my initial prayer. If the person I'm training is Tom, I will tell him to be ready to pray as soon as I look at him (another good reason to have your eyes open in prayer). After my introduction with the person we are praying for, I will say a short prayer and bless the person with the love of God (about 30 seconds). I will then look at Tom (or tap him on the shoulder if his eyes are closed) and he will then pray a quick prayer of blessing as well. When we finish up with that individual (we may have another quick prayer exchange for a follow-up), I will debrief with Tom about what he saw and heard during that encounter.

Again, this debriefing is critical to the discipleship process, as we can discuss and learn what God is doing and how to recognize and move in the gifts of the Holy Spirit. There is nothing quite like seeing someone experience God use them to bring healing or salvation to another for the first time in this type of setting. Soon, they will be ready to show others how to do it as well. That is not only discipleship, but multiplication! This is the way the Kingdom of God works. Do you need to find a mentor? Maybe you need to find a disciple. Either way, one is out there waiting for you.

Chapter 16

OVERCOMING DISCOURAGEMENT

In the neighborhood I grew up in, many of the boys had motorcycles. We would ride near our homes on the fire roads and irrigation trails. I was about fourteen years old and I wanted to fit in, so I bought a Kawasaki 90 Bushwhacker. Being the frugal family that we were, we found a bargain (we thought). It was a used dirt bike with what turned out to be a plethora of hidden mechanical problems. A week after I got it the engine seized, and that was the beginning of a long journey of repairing the bike with my dad. It took several months of working on weekends, and all the while my friends were out riding and having fun without me. It seemed every time we fixed something we would find another problem. I remember getting frustrated on numerous occasions with how hard and long we had to work to get the bike going again.

Added to this was the fact that my dad was an aeronautical engineer, and was somewhat of a perfectionist, to put it mildly. To him this project was a puzzle to be solved, and we had to do everything perfectly. No short cuts, no easy ways around it. When I would get exasperated and say something like, "This is taking forever! Can't we just get it done?" He would always say the same thing: "Nothing worthwhile is ever easy." Now this was not just a project, but a way for us to work and spend time together. At least that was how he saw it. It was also a way for him to assist me along the journey toward maturity. (We call this parenting). I was learning to overcome discouragement and frustration, even though I didn't sign up for that. To be honest, I'm still working on those lessons. I think my grade for that class would read "incomplete."

Likewise, in our journey of street and marketplace ministry, inevitably there will be times where things are not going well and discouragement could stop us from engaging in Kingdom ministry. I have shared many testimonies about miraculous healings and radical salvations, but these are just some of the highlights. The truth is that there are many low-lights as well. You will go through stretches where people are not being responsive, or no one seems to be getting healed or saved. Roadblocks are being put up to ministry, or team members are not showing up. There are days at a roadside "Need Prayer?" Booth where no one stops for ministry after we wait there for three hours! Or we pray for physical healing several times for an individual and there is no measurable result (that we can see).

It would be easy for me to give up and quit, but then I remember: Nothing worthwhile is ever easy. The two concepts that I feel the Lord has taught me through all of this is the importance of persistence and consistency. Persistence means that I keep at it and don't give up. *"...whoever sows to please the Spirit, from the Spirit will reap eternal life. Let us not become weary in doing good, for at the proper time we will reap a harvest if we do not give up"* (Gal. 6. 8b-9). Remember how I said prayer ministry is like going fishing? There will be times when we catch none. I don't let that stop me because I have seen the "whoppers": the salvation stories, the amazing healings, and the miraculous answers to prayer. They are out there in the streets. It takes persistence to push through the lulls to catch them.

Consistency means being available on a regular basis for God to use you to bless others. We try to set up our booth on the same day of the week, and at the same time of day. For example, most of our "Need Prayer?" Booths are weekly events, at the same street corner in a city on the same day and time (i.e. Thursdays, from 3-6pm). We commit to be there whenever possible, and not give up if there is a dry spell. We press through discouragement by acknowledging that God has sent us there, and He has told us that we will, in the long run, reap a harvest. If a door closes in one location, the Lord always seems to open up a better one. We keep pressing into healing and salvation, and in due season, they will come.

What keeps me going each time is the thought that God has appointments with people, and I want to be there when it happens. I want to position myself on a consistent basis to be at the right place at the right time. So often I have had people say to me it was a miracle that I happened to be on that spot offering prayer at that time for them. They say I wouldn't believe the circumstance that led them to that moment in time. All the while I'm thinking inside, "No, I really do believe it, because it is not a coincidence. I am here because the Lord told me to be consistent and persistent. The only miracle is that He chose me to be part of this." Then I smile at them and say, "God knows what you need. He had an appointment with you that you didn't even know about. Let's pray."

Chapter 17

DISCOVERING YOUR SPIRITUAL GIFTS

Hobbies are an interesting phenomenon. I'm not sure if everyone has a hobby, but those that do can tell you more about it than you would ever want to know on the subject. I think we pick hobbies based on what we enjoy and like to spend time doing. Hobbies are not work, but are activities that make us come alive. My hobby is collecting, restoring and playing pinball machines. I grew up in the 1970s during the golden age of pinball. The activity of pinball has always fascinated me, and I enjoy the challenge and competition of pinball playing. There is a whole sub-culture of pinballers, or pin-heads as we are affectionately known, and I find comradery with others who play in pinball leagues and tournaments. It is also a great way to meet people who don't have a relationship with Jesus. But I enjoy the hobby for its own sake because it gives me pleasure and makes me feel alive. That's not a bad thing, if you think about it. It's a gift from God, and if I keep it in the proper perspective in my life and relationships (my wife likes pinball too), it is a gift to be enjoyed.

What makes you come alive in ministry? What activity in serving others by the power of the Holy Spirit gives you pleasure and enjoyment? If you can pinpoint those, you are probably functioning in your spiritual gifts. One of the burning questions followers of Jesus often have revolve around the area of spiritual gifts. "What are my gifts from the Holy Spirit?" "Do I have gifts that I haven't discovered yet?" "How can my gifts be developed and matured?" "Can I move in the gift of prophecy?" "Do I have gifts of healing?" The Apostle Paul uses the strong language of imperatives (commands) when he says, *"eagerly desire the greater gifts"* (1Cor. 12.31) and *"eagerly desire gifts of the Spirit"* (1Cor. 14.1).

You might be asking what this has to do with street prayer and marketplace ministry. The answer is in two parts: We must be operating in the gifts of the Holy Spirit to be effective in this ministry, and secondly, we discover our spiritual gifts at a point of need. Attempting to do any Christian ministry without the gifts of the Spirit is like trying to drive your car somewhere without gasoline – you might look cool sitting in that Porsche, but you aren't going anywhere. In addition, you will discover and develop your spiritual gifts as you put yourself in position to need them. The beauty of the way God formed us is that when we are doing things in His Kingdom by the gifts of the Spirit, it will make us come alive and gives us great pleasure. It's not work, but enjoyable when we are functioning in the special way He had in mind when we were created.

This need and dependence on the gifts of the Spirit becomes very evident when you begin to pray for people on the street. Most of the people you will minister to have great needs, and you will feel very inadequate in your own abilities to really love and help them. But it has been said that 90% of ministry is the willingness to "just show up" and be available to God to bless others. It is at that point (in our weakness and obedience) that God can show Himself to be strong. This is where we, as well as the person we are ministering to, really need God to do what He does best: break in with his Kingdom of righteousness, peace, and joy in the Holy Spirit (Rom. 14.17). He will do that by releasing through us the gifts of the Holy Spirit.

Doing street and marketplace ministry is an ideal environment for discovering and developing your spiritual gifts. If you do this for any length of time, you will quickly find that this is a "God-sized" job, and that you really need Him to show up! The wonderful thing is, He always does. In fact, the Lord delights to come with His love and power in situations where it's impossible to be effective without Him. It has been said that "Faith" is spelled "R-I-S-K." Putting ourselves out there in the street is risky, but it is also positioning us to be used by God to bless others with the gifts of the Holy Spirit. Gifts are not given to us by God in a vacuum. If we are on our own and isolated, there is little need for us to be gifted and empowered by the Holy Spirit. A hermit in a cave somewhere is not going to need the gifts that are given "for the common good" (1Cor. 12.7). In other words, these gifts are given to us to bless others. We will only need them if we are ministering to other people.

Some of the common gifts I see that are needed and released in this setting are: healing, prophecy, discerning of spirits, miracles, faith, knowledge, wisdom and compassion. I believe there is what have been called constitutional and situational gifting (gifts you operate in frequently and those you are given in the moment). While I think that is a valid concept, I have also found that God can do whatever He wants, whenever He wants; *"My purpose will stand, and I will do all that I please"* (Is. 46.10). It seems to me that a big part of what He wants to do is let His Kingdom come and His will be done, on earth as it is in heaven (Mat. 6.10). He does that primarily through sending out His people, filled with the Holy Spirit and moving in spiritual gifts.

Do you want the gift of healing? Go where people are hurting and start ministering to them. Do you want to prophesy? Find individuals who need to hear from God and are looking for help. Would you like to see real miracles happen, but have never actually seen one occur? Position yourself in situations where only a miracle will do. These are the people and places where God is known to show up. He can do some great stuff inside the church, but it is only a hint of what He will do outside where the least, the last and the lost are located. That is why the church needs to "leave the building." We see that Jesus did works in the synagogue, but most of the real Kingdom ministry and miracles happened outside with the common people. He was known to hang around with all the "wrong" people, and yet it was among the "unclean" that His power came through the strongest. And He did His work by the power of the Holy Spirit. *"And the power of the Lord was with Jesus to heal the sick"* (Lk. 5.17). Let's follow that example.

Chapter 18

THE SEVEN WORDS THAT CAN CHANGE SOMEONE'S LIFE

For many people, the words "Will you marry me?" will change their lives forever. In my case, I asked Pam to marry me after we had dated for more than a year. By the time I got down on a knee and proposed I was very confident that she would say "yes." We fell in love and had a long courtship, but I think from the beginning I knew I would marry her, or at least that was my desire. So even though I formally proposed (I'm old fashioned that way), it wasn't that I "popped the question" as if marriage was a surprise. There was in time a gradual mutual understanding that we loved each other and that the Lord was putting us together as a couple. It took her some time to come to the same conclusion that I had, but eventually she saw the light. We have been married now for over 35 years.

For me the real tension came when I knew I had to ask her father for his blessing to marry his daughter. I was scared to death! I didn't really have much of a relationship with Gerry, and he was very aloof toward me. Some of that was my fault for sure, but I was raised in a family culture where the proper thing to do was to get his blessing for the marriage. I didn't want to do it, but I had to do it. I had to speak words to someone that might have life changing implications. What if he said no? What if he laughed at me? What if he gave me a lecture on what he was looking for in a husband for Pam and how I didn't measure up?

A plan formed in my mind: I needed to get Gerry away from his house, because he was always watching television when he was home from work. I couldn't imagine asking him for his blessing while he was absorbed in *Magnum P.I*! I decided to invite him to a college basketball game, and I would ask for his blessing there. The original idea was to get it over with right away, but I couldn't pull the trigger on the way to the game in the car. I was very nervous and my head was spinning! The game came and went and I can't remember anything that happened except the burning desire to get the conversation over. But I still didn't ask him at the game, and panic was setting in. On the drive home the intensity continued to build, and a voice in my head was saying over and over again, "You are blowing this. You are running out of time. Just go ahead and ask him!"

As I was pulling off the exit from the freeway to his house I knew it was now or never, so I finally blurted out something like this: "Pam and I really love each other and we want to get married. I would like to have your blessing to marry your daughter." I'm sure it didn't come out that smooth, as I was exhausted from the inner struggle and relieved that I had got the words out. But then, when he responded, it almost made me laugh. "Sure, you guys can do whatever you want." That was as close to a blessing as we were going to get, and I think he was surprised that I had even asked. What I thought was a huge deal turned out to be no real big deal at all. I have to say I was kind of disappointed because of the big build-up I had given this in my mind, but I was also glad that it was over. And the best part was I had his blessing to marry the woman I loved.

Words can be life changing, and I believe God is providing opportunities all the time for us to see lives changed. Wherever we go as followers of Jesus, we will meet people: at work, at school, at the store, in the neighborhood. These are people who are created in the image of God and were made to glorify and enjoy Him forever. Some have a relationship with Jesus and some don't yet. God wants to change all of their lives. As ambassadors of the Kingdom of God, how do we minister the love and power of Jesus in the street and marketplace to these people with whom we come into contact? One way is to ask people how they are doing and what is happening in their lives. Now if we really listen to people's stories it gives us an opportunity to offer to pray for them. Prayer can be a way into their lives, if we will ask. If we make an offer to pray, many will think we mean we will pray for them when we go home or to church. The key is to get them to allow us to pray for them right then.

The seven words that can change someone's life are: "May I pray for you right now?" Some will be too stunned to say "no," and others will feel it would be awkward to refuse such an offer, so many will say "OK." (I will detail what to do if they say "no" in the next chapter). The moment they give their consent I go right into the prayer. I pray the love of God over them as well as any request or need they have mentioned. I keep the prayer short, usually under a minute, and I pray with my eyes open to see what they are doing and what God is doing.

For example, if I'm talking to my neighbor, John, about how his family is doing, he might mention a problem he is having with his son. If asked, he might allow me to pray right then for him and his situation. Whether John is a believer or not doesn't really change the way I would pray in the moment. The prayer might go like this: "Lord, thank You for loving John and caring about him and his family. I pray You would give him wisdom in how to best restore his relationship with Travis. I pray You would let Your love and forgiveness win in this difficult situation. Thank you that John is Your son; You love and delight in him. Bless him now with that love, in Jesus name, Amen." Notice again how many times love is mentioned in this prayer. Love is the key! It is amazing to see what the Holy Spirit can do in such a short prayer exchange. He can do more than we think because He loves these people and is not limited by time.

Another exciting aspect of this offer of prayer has to do with healing. When I meet and talk to people they often have medical or health issues that are obvious or reported in the conversation. This is an opportunity for the Lord to show that He is present and bring the Kingdom of God in healing the sick. I may even ask, "Do you have any health problems or concerns that I can pray for?" Then I ask, "May I pray for you right now?" and when they say "yes" I go right into a prayer for healing. Again, this is a short prayer exchange for healing, where I ask the Lord to right whatever is wrong. This can also take the form of a prayer of command where I speak with authority for the condition to be removed. All this is done in a calm, conversational voice, assuring the individual of God's love for them. I then ask them how they are feeling and measure any results of the prayer exchange. It is always a great blessing to see how often God delights in healing people outside the walls of the church! Many who are touched do not yet know the Lord, or are far off in their walk with Jesus (prodigals). A simple offer of "May I pray for you right now?" can be the spark that helps an individual encounter God and have the course of their life changed forever.

You don't have to be in an organized ministry like the "Need Prayer?" Booth to do this. Wherever we go there are people who need a touch from God. The workplace, marketplace, neighborhood, and school are all potential points of contact to bring the Kingdom of God. If we are willing, we can meet people, listen to their stories, and then ask, "May I pray for you right now?" Being kind, compassionate and a good listener will go a long way in opening up many doors for this kind of ministry to take place wherever we go. At first, those seven words may be hard to get out of your mouth – like the words I needed to say when I was asking for my future father-in-law's blessing. But as the Holy Spirit prompts you, you will in time be able to say to just about anyone you talk with, "May I pray for you right now?" That will be the start of a grand adventure in the greater story of God. Now somebody who just read this is going to do this soon, and God is going to show up big time!

Chapter 19

THE POWER OF THE BLESSING

Some years ago we did an organized healing ministry at our church. People would come on Wednesday nights and sign up to have a team of people pray for them in one of the offices or classrooms. It was a wonderful ministry, and our teams witnessed God's work in powerful ways. One night a woman asked for prayer and was assigned to the team I was leading in one of the classrooms. I don't recall her specific prayer request, but I do remember that she was about 30 years old, and looked very unhappy. During the prayer I sensed the Lord saying, "She needs a father's blessing." I told her what I felt that God told me and asked if it would be all right if one of our team gave her a father's blessing. Coy was part of my team. He was a big teddy bear of a man, 65 years old, bald, gray, and about 300 pounds. He also exuded the love of God in a very tangible way.

I asked Coy to give this woman a father's blessing. What happened next was remarkable. He took her hands, looked her in the eye and said something like this: "Laura, I'm so proud of you. You are so special to Me and I love you so much. I bless you with all of My heart. I want you to know that I'm not disappointed in you at all, but I delight in all of who you are." By this point she was sobbing and shaking and smiling all at the same time. They embraced for what seemed like ten minutes and it was obvious that the Heavenly Father was healing her heart. Toward the end of the embrace she whispered in Coy's ear: "Thank you for blessing me. I love you too." I think those words were intended more for God than for Coy. She reported later a major breakthrough in her life with freedom from depression and fear.

"Your father's blessings are greater than the blessings of the ancient mountains, than the bounty of the age-old hills" (Gen. 49.26). There is great power in a blessing, and it is probably more than we know. Everyone is looking for a blessing, whether they realize it or not, and God has called His people to be a blessing to all the nations of the earth (Gen. 12.2-3). When we minister to people on the street and in the marketplace, we have been given the commission to bless them. This works very practically in an exchange with individuals for whom you offer to pray.

Sometimes, when you say the seven words that can change someone's life ("May I pray for you right now?"), they will say "no." They will usually be polite, but express they are not ready for prayer. When I first started out doing the "Need Prayer?" Booth, especially in the marketplace, when someone said "no," that usually ended the conversation. But as I did this more and more, the Lord gave me a key that would unlock many more Kingdom encounters with people. That key is the "blessing." Now, when someone says "no thanks" to an offer of prayer, I say "How about a blessing? Would it be all right if I said a blessing over you?" Surprisingly, almost everyone will say "yes!" "Prayer" means different things to different people, but a "blessing" is always a good thing! To me, a "blessing" is a prayer, but for some reason, people are more open to a "blessing," and this gives the Holy Spirit an opening to reveal the love and power of Christ.

This idea to offer a blessing first started when I was doing a prayer booth at a street market in Fullerton, California. We rented a space next to about a hundred other vendors selling everything from organic produce to time-shares. Our sign simply said, "Need Prayer?" The marketplace was different than our other road side locations, as hundreds of people would walk by in the course of the evening. While some would stop at the booth and ask for prayer, we found it was much more fruitful to talk with the people passing by and engage some in conversation. We would invariably ask, "May I pray for you right now?" Some would answer, "No, I'm good" or "Not right now." We learned to then say "How about a blessing?" Or "Could I say a blessing for you?" More often than not, the "no" now became an "okay."

So after their consent what do you do next? Begin speaking the blessing. If I am talking to Jeff, I will say something like "Lord, I ask you to bless Jeff right now. I bless his life and his work. I bless his finances and his family. Let him know how much You love him and that he is Your son, that You love him, and that You are delighted in him all the time. I pray this in Jesus' name, Amen." You will notice that this "blessing" is very similar to the prayer I pray in "How to Pray the Love of God." It is a very short blessing, but it is amazing what God can do in a person's spirit in that little opening. Often this will lead to an opportunity to do more ministry of prayer, but I never feel the need to push past where they are in that "God moment." If we are in the marketplace, I will often see that same person again and again, and I am confident that the Lord is at work in them. The "blessing" is often just the starting point or intersection of the Holy Spirit's interaction with individuals on their journey toward Christ. Some will come back for more prayer or ministry as they are wooed by God.

Some other Christians have asked me, "Do you pray a blessing over unbelievers?" My answer is "Absolutely!" It is the job of the Holy Spirit to convict people of their sin. My job is to love and bless all who the Lord sends my way. Many of the people I minister to on the streets and in the marketplace have had negative interactions with Christians. They are surprised to interact with us and find that we are normal people who love and want to bless them. I trust that God is drawing people to Himself, and I try to bless those He wants to draw into the Kingdom. I think there is a reason that they accused Jesus in His time of being "a friend to sinners." Jesus hung out with sinners, and touched all the "wrong" people. That is where He got His disciples, those who would change the world. Most of those people would not be found in the synagogue (the church). They are found outside when the church has left the building. That is where most of life happens. *"God demonstrates His own love for us in this: while we were still sinners, Christ died for us"* (Rom. 5.8). One of the best ways to demonstrate the love of God to others is to bless them. There is great power in the Father's blessing. And it is often the beginning of making disciples.

Chapter 20

WHO SHOULD DO STREET AND MARKETPLACE MINISTRY?

One of the main goals of writing this book has been to help train and equip people to be more effective in street and marketplace ministry. I want to take what I have learned and give it away so others can bring the love and power of Jesus outside the church walls and into the community. The objective is to motivate Christians to "leave the building" and reach out to people where they work and live. Some readers are already doing this. But if not, I hope to inspire you to take that first step out of your comfort zone and find God is with you as you take that risk. There is another great story about John Wimber and his response to people in the church who wanted more "meat" in his teaching and preaching. He said, "The meat is in the street!"

You might be asking, "Can I really do this?" Let me make a few observations about who can do this type of ministry. The qualifications are basic, yet profound: You must love Jesus and you must love people (Mat. 22. 36-40). This can be the only motivation to do this ministry (or any ministry for that matter) that will make it fruitful. Love is what it is all about, and the love of God in us is what will reach the world with the gospel. The perfect love of God will drive out the fear that keeps us in our western

Christian bubble. We will find the meat in the street if we are willing to say yes to God and take His love outside the building.

Ninety-five percent of the people I meet who want to do street ministry have this motivation, yet there are always a few with ulterior motives. I feel it is important to discuss this here because people with hidden agendas may want to join your team in outreach. Since this requires a team effort, it is important to know who you are partnering with in ministry. Some people are just not suited to do this.

The first ulterior motive is what I call the martyr syndrome. These people have a need to feel special or part of a small remnant, and this desire is reinforced as they are rejected or persecuted for taking a stand for Christ. Unfortunately, many groups that are out interacting with the public are either cults or fringe Christian groups. You may see such a group holding signs outside sporting events with a very polarizing message. One of the major obstacles in our interaction with people outside the walls of the church is to overcome this stereotype with our love and acceptance. We will suffer some persecution regardless for speaking about Christ publically, but let's make sure it is for being Christ-like and not for being weird, judgmental jerks.

Others have a desire to "build the church" and convince everyone they meet that their particular church or movement is the best. This is a sectarian spirit, and is the hallmark of cults. We want to avoid the classic bait and switch when we do public ministry. For example, some groups may offer prayer, but what they really want to do is get you to join their church. This is disingenuous at best and deceptive at worst. People will often ask you what church you belong to, but it is usually a check to see if you are in a cult. I only talk about "my" church if they are looking for a church home (and they live in the area). I make sure they know we are there to pray and bless them with no strings attached. When people on the street ask me what church I go to, I will usually say something like "I attend the Inland Vineyard Christian Church, but we have Christians from many different churches and denominations that do this ministry together." People seem to feel safer if it is not just one church participating because it sounds less like a sect or cult. That is just the reality of ministry on the streets.

Finally, some people just love to argue about doctrine, or want to "fix" the wrong thinking and behavior of individuals they meet on the street. My friend and mentor Jax use to call this a "fighting spirit." This tends to come from a prideful desire to let people know you are right and they are wrong. You can see this in less dramatic ways when your team members want to council or instruct people in these ministry settings. They attempt to correct their wrong thinking and therefore their wrong behavior by putting on the "parent" voice. Or they keep looking for something to disagree with so they can engage in a debate or dispute about the Bible. In the long run, this rarely ends well, and should be avoided whenever possible. Persecution, evangelism and sanctification will happen, but they are healthy bi-products of loving people with no other agenda than having them encounter a loving and powerful God as we pray for them.

So if your desire to do street and marketplace ministry is based on your love for God and your love for people, what do you do next? I would suggest you pray first and ask God for two things to begin with: a partner or two, and a location. The "Need Prayer?" Booth idea is not the only way to do it, but it is what I am familiar with, so I will detail the process with that ministry in mind. As you are praying for people and a location, talk to others about your vision and begin looking for a place to set up a "Need Prayer?" Booth. You have two main options: street locations (free), or marketplace booths (a weekly fee). Street locations: If you have church members who own a business locally where there is parking, that might be a place to start. You will need good visibility to traffic for your signs or banners, and a place for cars to pull in and park. Sometimes you can find an empty lot on a busy street to locate your booth. You might be able to obtain permission if you can contact the owner, but often it is easier to just try it out and see if anyone objects. Locations near hospitals are especially good, as you will get some action from the patients and family members.

Marketplace booths: You can also do a Prayer Booth at swap meets, downtown "open markets," as well as other public events like farmers' markets. Check with local officials for rules and costs. While the disadvantage is the cost of the marketplace, the advantage is that you will have more exposure to foot traffic, and will likely get to pray for many more people. The best locations are those where you can set up weekly, as consistency is key. (You will even get to pray for the other vendors and staff as you build relationships).

PART 2

TESTIMONIES

A NOTE ABOUT THE TESTIMONIES

God has been doing amazing things over the course of the last seven or so years since I started doing the "Need Prayer?" Booth. As I said before, I don't feel that it is much of an exaggeration to say that I have seen more people get saved and healed in the past seven years than in the previous 30 years of following Jesus. In including these testimonies here, it is my desire to share with as much accuracy and integrity as possible what actually happened. These are eyewitness accounts of what God has done, and with a few exceptions, I was the one privileged to see this with my own eyes. (I do report a few testimonies from my good friend, Steve Collins, who has been a partner in the ministry from almost the beginning). We attempt to record in a journal the prayer exchanges we have with individuals at all of our locations, and these records have been invaluable in recounting the stories and details of these events. At some of the marketplace locations we have so many people getting prayer that it is difficult to record promptly all that has occurred, but memory serves well when remarkable things happen.

Some of the names are not recorded, as a courtesy to those involved, but whenever possible the names are the real people who have experienced God's love and power. It is also important to point out that these testimonies are only highlights from the thousands of prayer exchanges that have occurred over the past seven or so years. I do not intend to give the impression that every prayer brings this kind of dramatic result, for that would not be accurate. Not everyone we pray for is healed, and not all with a request get their prayer answered in the way they were hoping. But it is my conviction that every time we pray with people, something good does happen, and that good begins with the love of God.

One of my favorite scriptures is Romans 14.17. (You can tell because of how many times I have referred to it in this book.) It states that the Kingdom of God is righteousness, peace, and joy in the Holy Spirit. I believe that one or more of these good things happen every time we pray with someone. Righteousness is right standing with God and others, and is relational in its nature. It means God is putting things right. This could be anything from restoring a strained relationship with a spouse to a person receiving salvation from God for the first time. Peace is an awareness of God in the midst of circumstances, and a revelation that He is in control of our present and our future. Joy in the Holy Spirit is a super-abundance of the gladness of God in spite of circumstances, and is the result of an outpouring of the person of the Holy Spirit. All of this is the Kingdom of God being manifest, and I believe this is what happens when we pray for an individual and say to God, "Let your Kingdom come."

SYLVIA RECEIVES SALVATION, HEALING, DELIVERANCE AND JOY

A young woman parked her car next to the dirt lot where we had the "Need Prayer?" Booth set up in Corona, and got out with her 3-year-old daughter. She introduced herself to me and Steve Collins as Sylvia, and said she saw our sign and knew right then she needed to stop for prayer. She had just been released from rehab for methamphetamine addiction, and she was afraid she would go back to using again. Her addiction and drug use had almost destroyed her life and her family. She looked very young (early 20s), and her daughter was clinging to her side as she spoke. I felt prompted by the Lord to ask her if there was ever a time in her life when she had received Christ as her savior. She reported that she had not, but that her mother was a Christian, and had been praying for her.

We talked about the 12-step program, and how it speaks of a "higher power" that exists to help us. I told her that it is referring to Jesus, and that receiving Him into her life was the best place to start her new life being clean. I asked her if she was ready to commit all of her life to Christ, and she said "yes." I led her in a prayer of salvation, and when we were done, I asked if I could pray for her healing from addiction. I explained that brain chemistry and physiology changes with drug abuse, and that she would be fighting an uphill battle against addiction unless God healed her brain. I asked if I could lay hands on her head, and as I began to pray for God to reset the brain function back to how it was before she ever used drugs, I noticed that her face began to distort. She was grimacing and her whole body became rigid. Even her 3 year-old daughter noticed that something was wrong. I said to her at this point in a very calm voice, "There is obviously an evil presence here, and it is connected with your drug use. Do you want to get rid of this?" She said "yes," so I led her through renouncing the drug "spirit" (the Greek word here is *Pharmakeia,* which translates into the English word "sorcery" but is the root word where we get the word "pharmacy" or "drugs"), as well as the "spirit of death." She willing confessed sin, repented, and renounced the practice of looking to have her spiritual needs meet in an illegitimate way. She was delivered and set free right away as the spirits left.

I shared with her about how Jesus taught us that when unclean spirits leave we need to fill the empty place with the Holy Spirit (Mat. 12.42-45). I told her there was one more thing that I felt God wanted to do that day, and that was to fill and empower her with the Holy Spirit. She prayed and asked God to do this, and then in a few moments she began laughing! It was clear that the evidence that she was being filled was the release of incredible joy. I then remembered that she had told me about her mother praying for her, so I asked her to call her mom on her cell phone and tell her what had just happened. I can only imagine what that mother experienced as her prodigal daughter told her something like this: "I just received Jesus Christ as my savior, got healing from my addiction, got delivered from demonic spirits, and then was filled with the Holy Spirit and with joy!"

God had indeed done great things that day for her (Ps. 126.2), and there was much joy to go around. After Sylvia left, Steve and I just looked at each other and started laughing again, as we wondered, "Did that really just happen?" This prayer exchange was unusual in that God usually has only one thing on His agenda for a prayer appointment. But in this case it seemed He was giving grace for much more. In some ways the Holy Spirit was leading to the point where one step just led to the next, and the young woman was very willing to go through the process. What could take years for some people to experience, she received in less than half an hour! Again it's that verse of Romans 14.17 that says *"The kingdom of God is ... righteousness, peace and joy in the Holy Spirit."* When the Kingdom of God broke in for Sylvia that day, she received all of that. .

MAKING A "HOUSE-CALL"

Toward the end of the day at the "Need Prayer?" Booth, a woman came over to Steve and me and asked for prayer for her daughter. She explained that her daughter was ill and lived in Colorado, but could we pray for her here in California? After we did that, I asked her if there was anything we could pray for her personally. She said that she was a teacher's aide at the Juvenile Hall, and that she needed patience. As we began to pray the love of God over her, I noticed tears were starting to come down her face. When we finished, I asked her what was happening, and she reported that she sensed the presence of God in a very real way. She then said, "You have to come and pray for my husband!"

It was getting dark, and it would be too late for her to get him there, so I said, "We usually don't do this, but how about we make a house-call?" She thought that was great, but when I asked her to call her husband on her cell phone, she insisted he would be fine with the idea and just asked us to follow her to her house. We packed up the Prayer Booth rig and followed her into the hills. When we got to the house, I asked her to go inside and tell her husband what was going on, but again she insisted that everything was "fine." As we followed her into the house, she called out, "Honey, I brought some men with me to pray for you!" He was sitting at the dining room table and looked up at us with a surprised expression on his face that seemed to be saying, "What the heck are you doing in my house!" I quickly realized that I had about ten seconds to explain, so I said something like, "We do this prayer booth in a lot down by the hospital and your wife asked us to come over here and pray for you." Somehow this seemed to make sense to him, and we all sat down at the table and talked for a few awkward moments. His story was that he had had a motorcycle accident about a year previous, resulting in significant lower back pain. This pain kept him from doing most things, including the thing he loved most: flying airplanes.

I asked if we could pray for his healing, and he said "yes." I prayed and Steve prayed, and then we asked how he was feeling. He said he felt "fine," but then I asked him to move his lower back around and see if it was "better, worse or the same." He said it was the same and there was still pain. I asked to pray a second time, but afterwards he checked it and again said there was no improvement. By this time I started to get a little nervous and uneasy, but I pressed in and asked if I could pray a third time. He looked at me with sympathy and agreed. As I was praying the third time, I was sending out an S.O.S. silently to God, "Lord you brought us here and nothing is happening! This is embarrassing, and I don't know what to do."

At that very moment the Lord dropped some information into my spirit. He said to me in a still, small voice, "He hasn't forgiven himself." I stopped the prayer and asked if he was blaming himself for the accident and his injury, and he replied that indeed he was daily beating himself up over what had happened. I asked about the circumstances of the accident, but he couldn't even remember due to a concussion he suffered in the collision. I then asked the $64,000 question: "Have you forgiven yourself?" You could hear a pin drop in the room, and then he finally replied, "No, I haven't." At that point I said, "Well, I think that is why God sent us here," and began to lead him in a prayer to forgive and let himself off the hook. He repented for that sin, and confessed that he was depressed and felt like his life was over. The power of the Lord was present during that prayer in the same way it was for his wife when we prayed the love of God over her. There were tears coming, even though he was trying hard to fight them off. We got up to leave and they both thanked us for coming. As Steve and I were going down the walkway to our cars, I overheard him turn to his wife in the doorway and say "I have no pain in my back right now."

The next week both husband and wife came to the Prayer Booth. He testified that his back was totally healed and that he had mowed his own lawn for the first time since the accident, and he did it twice as fast as his the neighbor who had previously mowed it for him. The next question out of his mouth was, "What church do you go to?" We gave them a card with the church's name and address and they were there the next Sunday. That was about two years ago and they have been in the church ever since. About six months after they started coming to our church I found out that they had been Mormons. He had even gone back to the Mormon

Church and told them how God had healed his back. The congregants told him it was the devil who had done that!

The husband is now helping us pray for others as we give out food to the poor in our Manna House outreach, while his wife teaches the children about Jesus. Whenever I see them I am in awe of how God intersected their lives. They are a testimony of God's power to heal, save, and set free. Doing that "house-call" was way out of our comfort zone, yet it was clear that God was leading all the way. How wonderful to find ourselves in the center of God's will, helping people keep an appointment in the heavenly calendar that they didn't even know they had. *"In Him we were also chosen, having been predestined according to the plan of Him who works out everything in conformity with the purpose of His will"* (Eph.1.11).

IRENE'S KNEES HEALED

Eighty-something Irene came to the Fullerton Street Market to buy flowers. We had our "Need Prayer?" Booth set up alongside some fifty other vendors. There was a team of people praying for whoever wanted prayer, and Irene stopped to see what we were doing. It was clear that she was not expecting to see prayer happening in the marketplace, so I asked her if she needed prayer for anything. She said she didn't, but kept looking at the prayer activity going on in the booth. I then asked her if I could say a blessing over her, and she said, "Yes, a blessing would be nice." I had a young woman with me from one of the churches we were training to do this ministry, and we both took turns saying a blessing over Irene.

After about two minutes of that I asked her if she had any health issues or medical concerns for which we could pray. She complained of strong pain in both knees, making it hard for her to walk the length of the street where the market is held. She said she had arthritis in her knees and that little cartilage remained. I asked her if we could pray for her healing and she said "yes." I wanted to use this opportunity to train the young woman in the process of praying for healing, so I had her do the prayer as I coached her. I asked my partner, "What do you want the knees to do?" She said she wanted them to be better, but I asked her to be more specific. "I want the knees to function properly and the cartilage to be restored. I want all the pain to leave the body." I instructed her to speak to the knees just like she was talking to a person, and she did. (This young woman had never seen a healing or ever prayed for healing before).

All of this was occurring outside the booth, in the walkway of the market as dozens of people walked by. I then told Irene to try bending her knees to see how they felt. Starting slowly at first, her mouth dropped open as she realized that Jesus had really healed her. She said, "No pain! No pain!" and began doing deep knee bends. Her face got very excited and she started jumping up and down and shouting, "It's a miracle, it's a miracle! No pain! No pain!" Everyone in the market who was nearby stopped to look and see the spectacle of an 80-something-year-old woman jumping up and down shouting "It's a miracle!"

I felt like I was back in the book of Acts, as this was truly a sign and a wonder. The young woman was dumbfounded, and couldn't believe her eyes. We eventually brought Irene over to the booth and talked about her faith and her life story. She had emigrated many years ago from Romania, and wore a cross around her neck. She stayed with us for most of the remaining time in the market, and continued to observe as we prayed and ministered to the patrons of the market. *"Stretch out your hand to heal and perform signs and wonders through the name of Your holy servant Jesus"* (Acts 4.30).

A SKEPTIC'S CYST HEALED

We were set up at our weekly "Need Prayer?" Booth at the street market in Fullerton, and a few team members were sitting inside the canopy praying for one of the patrons of the market. A young man in his twenties was passing by and noticed our booth and stopped to look in. I was standing nearby, and introduced myself. He asked me what was going on, and I replied that they were praying for healing. He had this skeptical look on his face, and then said, "Oh, you can do that? I have a painful cyst on my right foot. Can you heal that?"

I could tell by the way he was phrasing things that he was not a believer and that he was somewhat mocking what we were doing. I felt the prompting to go ahead and engage with this young man, so I said, "I can't heal anything, but Jesus is able to heal. Would you like me to pray for your healing?" He said "sure," but it was apparent that he was just humoring me. I jumped right in and prayed, "Lord Jesus, let Your Kingdom come." Then I spoke a word of command, telling the cyst to fall off and all the associated pain to leave. This took all of 30 seconds, and he said to me, "That's it?" I asked him to move the foot around and see if anything had changed, but he said it felt the same. During this whole exchange I had the clear sense that the Lord was doing something in this guy's life, so I told him to come back in another week and see us again. He left and I went on to pray for others that evening.

The next week I was at the market early, and while I was still setting up the booth, out of the corner of my eye I saw this same young man running toward me. The look on his face was very different than when I had seen him before. He looked surprised, yet curious. He said, "Do you remember me?" "Sure" I replied. He told me, "You wouldn't believe what happened." I had a good idea what had happened, but I said "Try me." "That cyst fell off this week all by itself," he replied, "and all the pain is gone! How did you do that?" This is what is known as a teachable moment, to say the least. I began to explain that it wasn't I who had healed him, but the Lord. "Let me tell you about Jesus," and I went on to share the gospel with a person that was now willing to listen. I would like to tell you that he dropped to his knees and got saved right then, but that didn't happen. He was on a journey towards Christ, and this was a seed that was sewn into good soil. It is the Holy Spirit who "closes the deal," and I had to be okay with the idea that he wasn't ready in that moment. I don't know what happened to him after that, but I feel confident that God is at work in that young man.

AC REPAIRMAN RECEIVES MINISTRY

Opportunities arise to pray and minister to people even when we are not looking for them. This can happen when we are going about our daily routines and then just recognize the divine set-ups that God is making available. It was summer in Riverside where I live, and the temperature was close to 100 degrees. My air conditioner at home went out, so I had to get it repaired promptly. I called the company that had installed the unit, and they sent over a repairman named Chris. I invited him into the house after he was done with the job to fill out the paperwork and have a glass of water. As Chris was writing up my bill, his cell phone rang and he later told me that it was his mother. She was worried about a biopsy he was scheduled to have later that day on some lymph nodes. The doctors were looking for potential cancer.

In that moment I felt the nudging of the Lord to pray for Chris. This is the moment of faith (spelled R-I-S-K) where I have to decide if I will go for it, even if it feels awkward. So I said, "Could I pray for you right now?" I kept the prayer short, but asked the Lord to pour out His love and peace on Chris, and to let the perfect love of God drive out fear. When I was done, I could see that Chris was visibly shaken and impacted by the presence of God in the room. He couldn't say anything for a while, so we both just sat there and soaked in the holy moment. He finally said, "I was not expecting that today. But I really needed it. I have a peace now that everything is going to be okay." I told him that it was not a coincidence he was assigned by the company to be the repairman for that particular job on the same day he was scheduled to have a medical procedure done.

Chris had a real encounter with the love and power of Jesus in the middle of his workday, and it was scheduled by God in His heavenly calendar. For me, the sting of the repair bill was more than outweighed by the feeling of joy I had to be the one who could help Chris keep his appointment with God. As Chris left and my house began to cool off, I couldn't help but think to myself, "Isn't God cool!"

FAMILY IN TURMOIL GETS HEALING AND SALVATION

I was standing on the edge of the "Need Prayer?" Booth at the Fullerton market, asking God to send more people my way. As I was looking at the passers-by, I sensed the Lord highlighting a couple as they walked right past me. I usually don't do this, but I felt a nudging, so I called out to them, "Hey, do you guys need any prayer?" They stopped and I could see they were huddling and discussing whether they should let me pray for them. They finally walked over and said, "Yeah, we could use some prayer." They were a married couple in their thirties, and he needed a new job. I brought another team member from the booth over, introduced everyone, and then we prayed for the husband first.

As I was praying for him, I noticed that the wife began to weep. As we finished the first prayer I asked her what was happening. She explained that she was a Christian, but had not been walking with the Lord for quite a while. Through tears she said that she was very depressed and even medication didn't seem to help. She felt ashamed and worthless, but experienced the presence of God for the first time in a long time as we were praying for her husband. At that moment God gave me what I would call a gift of faith. It is a supernatural confidence that something miraculous is about to happen. This is very situational, and is not something I or anyone else I know walks around experiencing all the time. But when it comes, it is always very exciting. So I said to her, "I think Jesus wants to do something about your condition right now."

I then invited the Lord to bring his Kingdom and I told the depression and any dysfunction in the brain to leave. After a short prayer (not really a prayer so much as a command), she was filled with the Holy Spirit and joy. Something radical changed in her, and was apparent all over her face. She was literally beaming. As she was talking about how great God is, I noticed another woman and a young boy standing behind us, observing very closely what had been happening. They turned out to be her sister and nephew.

The sister had brought her son out from St. Louis to live with the woman and her husband because of difficulties with her other son.

Everyone was introduced, and then I asked if I could pray for the sister. The first woman, who was no longer depressed, but now filled will the Spirit to overflowing, said "I want to pray for her!" She prayed with fire and passion over her sister like it was Jesus Himself who was praying. She was so full of faith and full of God that the sister was blown away. She too began to weep, and her son started hugging her around the waist. (All of this was happening out in the marketplace where the foot traffic was and not in the booth itself).

When she finished this amazing prayer (it was as much a prophecy as it was a prayer), I then asked the sister, "Has there ever been a time in your life where you received Jesus Christ as your savior?" Her reply was "No, I truly never have done that." "Would you like to do that right now?" I asked. Like fruit that is ripe and ready to fall off the tree, it was just a matter of catching her in the harvest. She of course said "yes," and I had the privilege of leading her in a prayer of receiving Christ. We then prayed a blessing over her son, and afterwards the whole family unit embraced right there in the middle of the market. There no doubt were angels in the middle of that hug too, and they were rejoicing!

A MAN WITH FLESH EATING BACTERIA

One day I got a call from one of the women in our church asking me to go pray for her brother-in-law who was in the hospital in Moreno Valley, California. This Hispanic man, in his early 40s, was dying of a very aggressive form of flesh-eating bacteria. When I arrived at the hospital, I found that the waiting room was filled with over 20 family members, most of whom were very solemn and grieving. I was introduced to the man's wife and children, and they thanked me for coming. I don't know what their expectations were for my visit, but I did feel a little like a fish out of water, only really knowing the sister-in-law. After meeting with the family, the hospital staff suited me up in very protective garb (which I was thankful for) so I could go in and pray for him. The man's wife went in with me, and when I got into the room I could see that the situation was very serious. The doctors had told the family that because the infection was caught late, there was very little chance of his survival, and that he most likely would not live through the night. They had already amputated one arm and part of his chest in an attempt to stop the infection, but were having little success. The family was told to make arrangements for his impending death.

There were doctors, nurses and technicians all busy around us and there was plenty of noise from the myriad of machines that kept his body functioning. With some level of apprehension I went in and laid hands on him (he was unconscious) and asked Jesus to touch him and bring the Kingdom of God. I told the infection to stop, and for the body to fight it off. I was thinking at the time that I had been sent by God to do this, so I was acting in obedience to Jesus' command to heal the sick. Did I feel great faith rise up in me? No. But I knew that the Lord had sent me, and I was to do my part. The rest was up to God. I have found that He is looking for people who are willing to say "yes" and be available to be used by Him in impossible situations. I tell people now that about 90 percent of ministry is the willingness just to show up. The other ten percent is made up of things like gifting, training, and experience.

I went back to the waiting room and prayed with the family. Again, I was not sure what they expected, and I was somewhat at a loss as to what to say to them, other than the truth that God was near to them and He was near to their loved one. About three weeks later I received another phone call. It was from the man's mother-in-law who was there when I visited the hospital. She again thanked me for praying for her son-in-law and thought I might want to know that he had recovered! Not only had his condition changed for the better immediately after the visit, but he made what she called a "miraculous recovery." In fact, he had returned home the previous week and was at that moment out riding his bicycle. A picture flashed into my mind at that second of this man riding a bike down the sidewalk with one arm! I couldn't help but laugh and rejoice with her on the phone and give thanks to God for rescuing this man from the brink of death. Some people have asked me if I have seen the dead raised. I reply, "No, but I have seen the near-dead brought back to life."

PRAYING FOR A COP WHO GAVE ME A TICKET

This story is a little embarrassing. It shows that you never know when and where you can be a blessing by offering prayer. I was leaving the Fullerton Street Market about 9 p.m. after doing the "Need Prayer?" Booth. We set up the prayer booth every Thursday during the market offering prayer alongside a hundred other "vendors" who sell everything from vegetables to real estate. I was driving home tired and not really paying attention after a long day of ministry. Suddenly there in my rearview mirror was a Fullerton motorcycle cop with his red light on! Bummer! I was going over the speed limit and he pulled me over.

I was thinking, "Great - no good deed goes unpunished" and feeling sorry for myself. After I showed him my license, registration, and insurance, the officer wrote the ticket, and as he was handing them back to me, he asked me what I was doing in Fullerton since I live in Riverside (about 40 miles away). I told him, a bit sheepishly, that I have a prayer booth at the Street Market on Whilshire, and then he said "Well, when you think about it, say a prayer for me." I said, without really thinking, "How about I pray for you right now? What is your first name?" He told me, so I started praying for this police officer standing right outside my car window! I blessed him for doing his job, and asked Jesus to reveal His love to him in a tangible way at that moment. I blessed his family and his finances, and prayed about some other personal things (based on some revelation).

He was visibly moved and didn't speak for a while after I finished the prayer. He seemed stunned. This had obviously never happened to him before. (It was a new situation for me too!) He had just been touched by the Lord. He finally said, "You are a good man, Todd," shook my hand and then walked back to his motorcycle. I have to admit I was hoping that he would rip up the ticket (he didn't), but I was glad I had an opportunity to show God's love to someone else that day. I stayed parked in that spot for a while, not knowing if we were done, and he just stood there by his bike unmoving, so I finally drove off. I was still unhappy I got a ticket, but I was also rejoicing in how God allowed that situation to present an opportunity to bring the Kingdom of God for that man. I pay more attention to my speed now, but I also say a prayer for that guy whenever I pass the "scene of the crime" on my way out of Fullerton.

BUSINESS INCREASES THREEFOLD AFTER PRAYER

One of the blessings of having a "Need Prayer?" Booth in the marketplace is the opportunity to pray for other vendors. It's different than doing a street corner or parking lot booth because you tend to get more "prayer action" with people walking by, and you also can start to develop relationships with the other "vendors." We had just started helping another church get a prayer booth initiated at the Pasadena Farmer's Market and began some conversation with the vendor next to our prayer booth. He operated a knife sharpening service. My friend, Glen Taylor, asked if he could pray a blessing over him and his business. The man seemed a little hesitant at first, but eventually agreed.

Glen asked the Lord to bless this man and his business and to let him know that God loved him and his family. No sooner had he finished the blessing than people started to bring their knives and tools for sharpening in record numbers! The man was astonished, and reported that he had three times the number of usual customers. I later talked to the same man at the end of the market and when he told me about his increase in business, I related that God sometimes does things like that to get our attention. He said to me, "Well, He definitely has my attention now!"

MUSLIM MAN COMES FOR PRAYER FOR HIS ADDICTED SON

One day at a Corona location of the "Need Prayer?" Booth, a brand new Mercedes sedan pulled into the parking lot where we have the booth set up. A man who looked to be Middle Eastern and about 45 years of age got out and walked over to me. He was dressed in a very nice three-piece suit, and the very first thing he said to me was "I'm a Muslim, but I want you to pray that Jesus would save my son out of heroin addiction." Wow. I was more than a little surprised that he would come to us for prayer, but I could see in his eyes the sincerity and desperation. He then went on a monologue of why it was okay for me as a Christian to pray for him, trying to convince me of the appropriateness of this seemingly awkward situation. I finally stopped him in his apology and said, "I'm more than happy to pray for you and your son. I'm glad you stopped. Tell me about your situation." He seemed to relax some at that point, took a deep breath and then unfolded the story of his son's addiction. The boy (who was now about 20 years old) had been given everything he could have wanted, but became addicted to drugs, and was heading into his third stint of rehab for heroin. The father was heartbroken by his son's sin and depravity, and felt powerless to help him get free.

At this point I had nothing but compassion for this man, and as a fellow father of a son, I could feel his pain and anguish. I wasn't looking at a follower of Islam anymore, but a fellow father and human being in great distress over a lost son. We took each other's hands and he bowed his head. I prayed to Jesus, as he had requested, that He would save his son. I asked Jesus to be merciful to this young man and rescue him from out of the pit of addiction and bring him to salvation. I prayed for the father to receive hope and comfort from the Holy Spirit, and to be held close in the love of the Heavenly Father. (I didn't realize it at the time, but what I had prayed was a very Trinitarian prayer!) We wept together – two fathers with hearts crying out to God for the rescue of one father's son. There was a long silence after I ended the prayer, but it did not seem awkward anymore. We had connected on a very deep level (even a spiritual level), and I felt very privileged to be in that moment with this man and with the presence of God.

In the moments following I had a very clear sense from the Lord that nothing more needed to be said. This man had come with enough desperation to let a Christian into his world and receive prayer outside his religious worldview. He was clearly touched as well, and could only say through tears, "Thank you." As he drove away, there was a deep abiding peace that came over me and a feeling of awe and wonder at what God had allowed me to participate in with Him. It was one of those moments in life that surpass words or emotions, and I still consider it one of the most amazing events of my ministry. I don't know what happened to the man or his son, but I do know that the Kingdom of God came down on two fathers as we connected our hearts in that prayer exchange.

ATHEIST HIP HEALED AT HOMELESS SHELTER

A few years ago we were looking for a second Riverside location to do a "Need Prayer?" Booth. My friend, Steve Collins, had been getting a lot of people coming for prayer in poor areas of both Colton and San Bernardino, California, including healing and salvation. So, I went looking to find a place to set up our "rig" in the inner city area in my town of Riverside. Through another friend I came in contact with a pastor who oversees much of the homeless ministry in the city, including several shelters. When I inquired about setting up a prayer booth near one of the shelters in the urban center, it was suggested that we do the prayer ministry inside the homeless shelter itself! This was a new frontier, but God seemed to be opening the door, so we walked through it!

One of the first encounters we had with our prayer team in the shelter was a young man who asked if we would pray for him even if he was an atheist. He had observed us praying for some of the other residents, and wanted prayer for his hip pain. We said, "Sure, we would be happy to pray for you. That's not a problem." We did a short interview about his condition, and then prayed a blessing over him. We followed this up with a prayer commanding the hip to be made whole. The whole time we were praying, this young man's eyes were open and he was watching us intently. When asked what he had experienced during the prayer exchange, he reported "I may not believe in God, but I did feel loved and accepted by you. That's a better way for Christians to present God as opposed to preaching at people. And by the way, my hip does feel better now." He thanked us and left.

The next week he came back over to our prayer area in the shelter and said he wanted to tell us something. He reported he noticed while taking a shower that week that the muscles and joint of the hip seemed to be "growing and moving around." He couldn't explain it, but he couldn't deny it was happening, and that it was good. The third week he again approached our prayer team and requested more prayer. He was referring to himself now as a "doubter," as opposed to an "atheist." When we finished with the prayer exchange he had difficulty putting into words what he had experienced, but thanked us again for caring for him as a person. It seemed to be the combination of how he was being treated lovingly by the team in addition to the healing he was receiving that was turning his heart toward God. He left the shelter the next week, so we didn't have an opportunity to follow up. But there was no doubt in anyone's mind that the Lord was at work in this man's heart and life.

MAN REPENTS BEFORE WE CAN EVEN START THE PRAYER

An African-American man in his 40s stopped by the Corona location of the "Need Prayer?" Booth and asked for prayer about his need for finances and a new job. I introduced myself by name and he told me his. While I was listening to his story, and before I could even pray, the Holy Spirit seemed to fall on this man and he began to spontaneously repent. He suddenly said he hadn't been walking with the Lord for quite a while, but knew now that he needed to come back to Jesus. He began confessing his sins in detail and was visibly under conviction. He said, "I didn't plan to do this, but I need to get right with God now! I can't keep living like this, for I know that I'm called to be a man of God." He then prayed to re-commit his life to Christ in the most earnest fashion.

The funny thing about this was that I didn't have to say or do anything really, as the Spirit of God did all the work. Sometimes the presence of the Lord comes in such a way that people start to repent or move toward God without any assistance from us. In this situation I was primarily a spectator and a witness to what the Holy Spirit was doing in this man. He came thinking he would get prayer for a job, but when he got into the prayer booth God showed up! My part was just to listen and observe and say "yes" and "amen." I kept thinking to myself as he was repenting and confessing and returning to God, "I'm so glad I came today and offered prayer out here. If I had stayed home today I would have missed this amazing experience. What a day. Thank you, Lord!"

"Or do you think lightly of the riches of His kindness and tolerance and patience, not knowing that the kindness of God leads you to repentance?" (Rom. 2.4)

BANK TELLER REFERS A CUSTOMER TO OUR "NEED PRAYER?" BOOTH

Most people see the "Need Prayer?" signs as they drive by, or walk by our booth in a marketplace or street corner. But every once in a while someone comes for prayer because of a referral from a family member or friend who has been to our booth and been touched by God. This story is a little unusual because of the circumstances involved in the referral.

A woman went to her bank and confided in the teller about some difficulties she was facing in her family. The teller must have seen our booth on a regular basis, because she told the woman, "If you go down to the corner of Brockton and Arlington, there are some Christians across from Starbucks who will pray for you. They are there every Friday. Look for the big sign that says 'Need Prayer?'" The woman came right away (this was a Friday), and told us that she was referred by the bank teller (we still don't know who that is) to get prayer at our booth. We prayed for her to receive the love of God, and blessed her with the presence of Jesus.

This is another example of how important consistency is in this type of ministry. The woman may not have come back to receive prayer on another day if we hadn't been manning the booth that day. Her story also reminded me of what happened in the book of Acts: *"The Lord told him, 'Go to the house of Judas on Straight Street and ask for a man from Tarsus named Saul, for he is praying'"* (Acts 9.11).

A WOMAN HEARS THE NAME "GOD" IN THE MORNING AND DRIVES AROUND THE CITY LOOKING FOR HIM.

A mother of three found herself in a struggling marriage and with little hope. She was depressed and desperate for help but didn't know where to turn. This young woman woke up one morning with the name of God in her ears and on her lips. She reported that suddenly she knew God was the answer to her dilemma, and went looking for Him in her car! She just started driving around the city, being compelled to look for the God who was the answer to what she needed. Shortly thereafter, she spotted our "Need Prayer?" Booth on the corner of a busy street and knew she had found her destination.

This is what is known as a divine appointment of the highest magnitude, so as she detailed her story to us, we began to share with her the good news about Jesus and His love for her. We explained that she could know God by receiving Christ, and she was more than ready to do that right then. What a joy to pray with her to receive the life offered by Jesus Christ in that next moment. It again reminded me of the truth that God has the "ability" if we will have the "availability." The Lord brought His Kingdom into her life in a very dramatic and supernatural way that day. Confession, repentance, salvation and joy were the result of the divine intervention of the Holy Spirit in her life. *"For the kingdom of God is ... righteousness, peace and joy in the Holy Spirit"* (Rom. 14.17).

AFTER PRAYER FOR BACK PAIN, A WOMEN'S LEG LENGTHENS AND HER FOOT GROWS OUT

There are times when we pray for people and God does more than we ask. His desire is to bless people, and He will give them what they need, even beyond what they are seeking. One Sunday morning at our church, I was praying for the sick, as is our custom. During this "ministry time" a woman who I knew fairly well in the church came forward and requested prayer for healing from some nagging back pain. Being someone who has also struggled with plenty of back issues in my past, I had empathy for her plight, and was more than willing to pray to see God ease her pain.

As I was ministering healing, I sensed the Lord prompting me to check her legs to see if one was shorter than the other. (I had learned to pray for this kind of leg-lengthening from a wonderful leader named Terry Virgo.) With her husband standing next to her, I had the woman sit down on the front row to check her legs. Sure enough, one was about one inch shorter and so as we prayed, I spoke to the leg and it seemed to grow out and they became equal. She stood up and said that her back was feeling quite a bit better. The interesting thing is that she came back the next Sunday and reported that she had always had trouble buying shoes because one foot was a size 5 ½ and the other was a 7. That week she noticed that her foot had grown out and now they were both equal size! God is amazing, and did something wonderful and unexpected.

An interesting side note is that I prayed for another woman with a short leg in the exact same way, and experienced an unexpected result on the other end of the spectrum. This woman had significant back pain, and when I checked her legs, her left leg was at least an inch and a half shorter. She was also with her husband and a friend (first time visitors to the church), and I was ministering with Susan, another woman on our prayer team. When I told the leg to grow out, it instantly grew out equal to the other one. Susan also saw it and her eyes got big with surprise. But the surprise I got was when I had the recipient of healing stand up and check her back pain. She reported that there was no change – she was still in pain and it felt the same! I told her I saw her leg grow out, and encouraged her that God was at work in her life. She thanked us and left.

What happened? There are so many variables in healing that it is difficult to say, but there was no doubt in my mind or Susan's that the woman's leg grew! Other factors, unknown to us at the time, were obviously in play. I feel that given the same circumstances, I would not change how I prayed. I trust that God will sort out everything else, and I have to rest in the tension of the Kingdom that is "now and not yet." An answer, one that is not complete or fully satisfactory, is that God has information we don't have, and sometimes He shares this with us, and sometime He doesn't. I'm learning to be okay with that.

SUICIDE ATTEMPT FAILS; WOMAN IS BORN AGAIN THE NEXT DAY

There are no coincidences with God, and there are no chance meetings with His Kingdom. A young woman stopped in to our Corona "Need Prayer?" Booth and reported that she had a "bad night" as she had taken "a lot of sleeping pills," and was surprised that she had even woke up alive that morning. She told her story: how she "liked to be alone," yet was "often sad and depressed." She obviously had just made a suicide attempt, albeit a shaky one, and was looking for someone to talk to about it. She drove by the booth, saw the sign and said to herself, "I guess it can't hurt."

After listening to her story and giving her time to open up about her inner world, I shared with her the gospel, and how Jesus was inviting her into the family (the Trinity) she had been looking for all of her life. God was offering her a real life, and one worth living. I then asked her "Where are you on your journey with God?" She replied, "I know God is real, but I don't know what to do next." I was very privileged to lead her in a prayer of receiving Christ, and then she prayed to be filled with the Holy Spirit. She came to Christ willingly and freely, without any pressure or hype. She was just ready, and it was her day of salvation. Together, we then broke the power of depression and death over her life, as I led her in prayers of confession, repentance and renunciation. I assured her that with Jesus she would never be alone again, and encouraged her to join with us in the local church to live out her new life.

It is always a delight to help others who are lost find the One who created them and loves them. It is not hard to do if God has positioned you in the "right place at the right time." Just being out there and available to God makes much of this possible, as He is looking for people who are willing to be present with others in their time of need. This is not just a serendipitous circumstance or random occurrence, but rather a planned, sovereign appointment set by the Eternal God in His great plan of redemption. Finding our role in this bigger story of God is not as difficult as some might think. It often starts with just saying "yes" to His call to position ourselves to be with the people who need His love and power. Not surprisingly, those people are all around where we live and work and play. Some of them are only one step from death, and one step from real life. Here is a prayer that is both dangerous and exhilarating: "Lord Jesus, put me in position to meet and love those people." Then hold on, because God is looking for friends who will pray just that!

"You, Lord, brought me up from the realm of the dead; You spared me from going down to the pit...Weeping may stay for the night, but rejoicing comes in the morning" (Ps. 30.3,5).

A WOMAN WITH TOTAL DEAFNESS IN HER LEFT EAR IS HEALED

There are some creative ways to positon ourselves to be used by God to bring His love and power to people in need. One way we have done this is to simply offer prayer where the homeless and the poor are being fed. Our church has a ministry pantry that gives away groceries to needy families called the "Manna House." People hear about this mainly by word of mouth, and on some days there are over a hundred people in line. After people have gotten food, at the end of the line we offer prayer to anyone in need. It has been our experience in this situation, as well as our prayer ministry at the homeless shelter, that the poor are very in touch with their needs. It is also prime real estate for the Kingdom of God to break in!

One week when we were offering prayer at the end of the Manna House line, Irma received more than just "natural" food. She received some of the "children's bread of healing." (Mat. 15. 26-28). She came in with her mother, asking for prayer for a problem in family relationships. They were both Spanish speakers, so the whole dialogue was translated by a co-worker in the ministry, Patrick. After praying for her family situation, we asked if she had any health concerns, and Irma mentioned that she was born totally deaf in her left ear. I asked her if we could pray for healing, and she gave her permission.

The first time we prayed (prayer of command) and told the ear to open up, I asked if we could test the ear. I asked her (through translation) to cover her deaf ear with her hand and I then snapped my finger next to her good ear to get a baseline. Then I had her cover her good ear and did the same thing to the deaf ear. She got a look of surprise on her face and said she could hear "a little bit" for the first time in her life. She was quite astonished, but we pressed into more healing and prayed again, the same way, and then tested the ears again. This time she reported that her hearing in that ear was louder, and when we prayed a third time, she began weeping and said she could hear clearly. She estimated that her hearing went from zero (completely deaf) to about 60% in her left ear. All of this exchange was being translated from and to Spanish, yet it was obvious to all present that Jesus had done a creative miracle in this woman.

SALVATION WAVES

There are times and seasons when God seems to be doing a specific work in His Kingdom, and that work continues like a wave. Sometimes it is healing, where you see more than the usual number of physical healings, or sometimes it is salvation, where a series of prayer encounters lead to people giving their heart to Jesus. I recall one such season at the "Need Prayer?" Booth, where Steve Collins and I led nine people to receive Christ in less than a month in three different cities. It is hard to explain, yet God seemed to be doing His salvation thing in a special way, and we just rode the wave while it lasted. Neither of us considered ourselves evangelists, yet there was a real sense of harvest going on. I believe that God is looking for average people who are willing to say yes to His call. We just showed up and got to help midwife some humans into the Kingdom of God.

This wave seemed to start with a man who came to the Riverside location with a substance abuse problem. His drug use had led him down a dark path: He had lost his job, became separated from his wife and child, and was in despair and hopeless. He drove by a "Need Prayer?" Booth, stopped, and prayed to surrender his life to Jesus Christ. Getting born again and filled with the Holy Spirit is a real good place to start! He was just ready, and God met him with His love and power and gave him new life. We helped get him plugged into a local church and rejoiced with the angels over one sinner who had been saved. Little did we know this would begin the wave of similar encounters that would lead to salvation, one after another. I recall another exchange the same week with a young woman who had been struggling with depression and some relationship issues, and was just ready to surrender her whole life to Jesus. No apologetics, no argument, no pressure, no hype, no convincing were necessary, just a heart draw by the Holy Spirit to salvation in a moment of grace. Such a wonderful sense of peace came, and there was no doubt this was a divine appointment. *"They were glad and honored the word of the*

Lord; and all who were appointed for eternal life believed" (Acts 13.48).

When you are riding these waves, some unusual circumstances can occur. During this time, a secular drug and alcohol counselor suggested a client "get some prayer somewhere" in the course of the session. The young man in his twenties saw our sign that offered prayer, and stopped in, saying "This is convenient and surprising!" We listened to his story of alcohol dependency and rehab, struggle and relapse. His heart was open to God, and we talked about the gospel and his need for Christ. We prayed together and he was ready to commit his life to following Jesus. Idols were broken and new life came with the filling of the Holy Spirit. I remember being in awe of the Lord, as this was the third salvation in as many days at the "Need Prayer?" Booth, starting the previous week (Friday, Tuesday, Friday). My heart was so full of joy! I think I could hear heaven rejoicing, too.

"At that time Jesus, full of joy through the Holy Spirit, said, 'I praise You, Father, Lord of heaven and earth, because You have hidden these things from the wise and learned, and revealed them to little children. Yes, Father, for this is what You were pleased to do'" (Lk. 10.21).

We had the privilege of leading two more people to Christ three days later! A woman who was an admitted addict, came and said she "needed God," was soon praying to commit her life to Jesus, and vowed to seek help for her addiction. Less than a half hour later, a man came by and said he wanted to "get saved." He had recently witnessed a horrific traffic accident in which he was the first on the scene; there were several fatalities. He was so impacted by this event that he could not stop thinking about life and death. He too was soon praying to receive Christ and was invited to join our community of believers.

This is not an evangelistic outreach, per se, but seeing people saved is a natural bi-product of offering the love and power of Jesus in prayer in the public arena. People stop for prayer at our booths many times because they are in crisis. This crisis is often an open door for the Holy Spirit to bring salvation through a brief declaration of the gospel. The rest is just catching the fruit as it falls off the tree! The feeling I had during this season was like when I was a young man out surfing and someone in the line-up would see a big wave coming and yell "Outside!" All I can say is "More, Lord!"

"The harvest is plentiful, but the workers are few. Ask the Lord of the harvest, therefore, to send out workers into His harvest field." (Lk. 10.2).

INSTANTANEOUS HEALING
DURING PRAYER TRAINING

I was invited to do some training about the "Need Prayer?" Booth at a small African-American Pentecostal church in San Bernardino. Church members had heard about what we were doing and had stopped by one of our booths in the city. This church was about to launch a monthly outreach into the community to reach the poor and homeless with many other churches offering help (food, clothing, medical, job assistance, etc.) and wanted to offer prayer as well. The associate pastor contacted me and asked if I would meet with a team from the church and present a three-hour workshop to help them get started.

The highlight of the training happened when I asked for volunteers so I could demonstrate how we pray for healing on the streets. The associate pastor's wife wanted prayer for three herniated discs in her mid-back (thoracic). She had been injured in a fall at work and had been in constant pain for about nine months. This was a workers compensation case, and she was fed up with the system and red tape. She was also on medication for pain that would not abate. As she stepped forward at the training, I began doing the healing ministry like I do on the streets, giving commentary to the group as I proceeded. I told the team something like, "Now that I know what the problem is, I will speak to the back and tell it to straighten up." Then with my eyes open and not touching her in any way I said in a normal, conversational way, "In the name of Jesus I tell the back to realign and all the discs and vertebrae go back to normal. All associated pain, leave the body right now."

This took about twenty seconds, and then when I asked her to bend and check how her back was feeling I asked, "Is it better, worse or the same?" She started to move this way and that, and then she said, "Wait, let me try doing this." And then she touched her toes and stood up real fast. She then kept saying, "This is for real – I don't have any pain at all – this is for real!" When this type of instantaneous healing happens it tends to change the way the rest of the meeting goes! We never got back on the other topics, but there was a great enthusiasm now in the group to talk about healing and how they could do the same thing on the streets. During this whole time, the pastor's wife was still moving around and saying, "This is for real! I'm totally healed!" When I first started to minister in the area of healing, I was surprised when healing happened. After seeing so many people healed on the streets and in the marketplace, I'm now surprised when healing doesn't happen.

MAN'S LEG IS HEALED AS HIS WIFE'S SKEPTICISM IS CHALLENGED

A man and his wife, were attending a class by Dr. Bill Jackson called "Learning to Minister Like Jesus." I was assisting Jax in the class and we were doing a clinic where we listen for words from the Lord specifically for healing. We were waiting on the Lord in the quiet when I saw in my mind's eye a picture of a broken bone with the two ends overlapping each other. I shared this with the class and held up my right and left index fingers as an illustration of the bones I saw that were overlapping. Suddenly the woman said, "Oh my God, that's you !" (Referring to her husband). She looked very startled, but when He described how his lower leg was shattered in an accident when he was a young man, it began to make sense. He said, to this day, whenever he explains the problem he has in that leg, he holds his two index fingers exactly like I did.

Jax and I both prayed for the man's leg, and he reported back over the next few months that his leg was miraculously healed. It was strong and he no longer suffered pain from activities or pressure that in the past caused great discomfort. But the interesting part was that was his wife was a major skeptic when it came to healing. She kept asking him if he was sure the leg was really healed. This skepticism seemed to be finally resolved when the surgical scar on the leg from the original injury started to disappear over time. The top of the scar, which went from the lower knee to the ankle, began to fade away. It got to the point that one of his adult children saw him in his swim trunks and said, "Dad! What happened to your scar?" He later told me he felt the healing he received was more for his wife than it was for him. He got healed in his body, but she had her world view reoriented.

PART 3

TOOLS

How to Do a "Need Prayer?" Booth

A Prayer Booth is a shelter providing a public offer of free prayer to anyone in need. It is staffed by a few people from local Christian churches, and is usually located on the street or in a community area. It is an effective means of outreach whereby believers can demonstrate love and care for the community. In our setting we put up banners that say *"Need Prayer?"* on an EZ-up type portable shelter in various locations in the city, such as empty lots on busy streets, at farmers' markets and swap meets. Drivers or passers-by stop and ask for prayer. Our goal is that people will experience the love and power of God as we pray for them. It is our experience that they do!

The Purpose of This Guide

Some of what is presented here is a review of what has been previously discussed in this book. We want to provide you with the information and tools you need to start a Prayer Booth ministry in your own town or city. We want you to be successful from the start, learning from our victories, as well as our mistakes. We are confident that if you will take the step to offer prayer out in the community, you will see God bless people in tremendous ways, and witness firsthand His Kingdom breaking into this present age.

What You Need

1. A heart to reach out into the community. You will be praying for some people who would never enter a church to get prayer, so it will take some of us out of our comfort zone. This is where Jesus did most of His ministry, so let's go where He would go.

2. A location. You have two main options: Street locations (free), or marketplace booths (a weekly fee).

1. **Street Locations**: If you have church members who own a business locally where there is parking, that might be a place to start. You will need good visibility to traffic for your signs or banners, and a place for cars to pull in and park. Sometimes you can find an empty lot on a busy street to locate your booth. You might be able to obtain permission if you can contact the owner, but often it is easier to just try it out and see if anyone objects. (They seldom do, unless it is causing traffic issues). Locations near hospitals are especially good, as you will get some action from the patients and family members.

2. **Marketplace Booths**: You can also do a Prayer Booth at swap meets, downtown "open markets," as well as other public events like farmers' markets. Check with local officials for rules and costs. While the disadvantage is the cost of the marketplace, the advantage is that you will have more exposure to foot traffic, and will likely get to pray for many more people. The best locations are those where you can set up weekly, as consistency is key. (You will even get to pray for the other vendors and staff as you build relationships).

3. Signs or banners. We use the words *"Need Prayer?"* and it seems to work well to communicate what we are doing. Some other ideas might be *"Free Prayer"* or *"Get Prayer Here."* Keep it simple and clear. I don't recommend that you put the name of your church or ministry on the banner. We use an A-frame "Sempo" sign on the sidewalk in addition to two or three 2'x8' banners hanging from a EZ-up that all simply say *"Need Prayer?"* It is critical to have good signage, and this is the most costly part of the Prayer Booth start-up. (We started out cheap with hand-made signs, but found that the professional banners will last for years and look much better). The EZ-up is necessary not only for sign hanging, but to shelter you in sun and rain!

4. Some folding chairs. Get at least four chairs, preferably with a padded seat (you will be sitting for a while).

5. People to pray (and train). Recruit people who want to pray for others in the community, or are willing to learn. You don't need an army, but you do want a few like-minded people who will go with you. (More on this later under "Co-Op")

6. *A journal* to record the prayer exchanges.

Guidelines (do's and don'ts)

We are offering (advertising) to pray for people, so that is what we should do. Many who stop for prayer are in crisis, and they are being vulnerable. There is nothing worse than the old "bait and switch," so we don't want to use this time for any other purpose than our primary objective - prayer. By this we mean that we don't preach at people when they come, and we don't see this as an opportunity to recruit them to come to our church. *Our goal is that people will experience the love of God when we interact with them.* We ask them what they need prayer for and then we pray. If they ask about our church later and want more information we might give them a card (if they are not in a church currently), or if they seem ready to make a decision to follow Christ we would offer to lead them in a prayer of commitment, but we let them indicate their interest. We never push people or pressure them – prayer is the main thing we are about, and we trust that God will reveal Himself through the prayer exchange. We want people to feel loved and accepted. After that, we try to follow the leading of the Holy Spirit.

Some people want to know who you are and what the booth is about before they let you pray for them. We usually say something like *"We are Christians from (fill in the blank) Church here in town and we are offering free prayer to anyone in need."* We introduce ourselves by name and ask the person's name. We then ask, *"How can we pray for you today?"* or *"What would you like prayer for?"* As they explain their story, we listen to them at the same time we are listening to God. Some people will want to tell you their life story, but you only need a place to start. You want to spend more time praying than talking (with most people you have a 3 to 10 minute window). So get into prayer by saying something like, *"OK (say their name), let's go ahead and pray now – Father, I thank you for (say their name) and for bringing them here for prayer today..."*

We usually don't lay hands on the people we pray for because we want to be sensitive to how they feel about being prayed for out in public. One exception to this might be if you are praying for physical healing, and then you should ask permission first. We train our prayer people to pray with their eyes open so they can observe any response the recipient may have and to see "what the Father is doing." Most prayers last only a minute or two. We then ask for some feedback from the person being prayed for, such as *"What were you experiencing as we were praying?"* This helps us evaluate what happened and may focus us on a new direction of prayer. A decision may need to be made at this point if additional prayer is to be offered. If so, this second round of prayer should be brief. We generally follow the Five Step Healing Model (you can find this online).

We tell the people we pray for our prayer booth schedule so they can return to receive prayer again or give a report of an answer (see section on consistency).

Guidelines for the Marketplace

While the street corner or parking lot "Need Prayer?" Booth has the advantage of people coming up specifically for prayer, at the marketplace many are walking by and curious. There is a need to engage people as they stop and look, or even slow down as they stroll by. (Some will come right in and ask for prayer, but many won't.) It is a good practice to stand at the edge of the booth and say hello to these people, and begin a conversation. An easy way to do this is to say *"Hi, my name is (fill in the blank). What is your name? We are Christians from (local church name) and we are offering free prayer to anyone who might need it. Is there anything we can pray for you about?"* About 80% of the people will say something like, *"No thanks, I'm OK."* We have found the key phrase is to say *"OK, how about a blessing? Would it be all right if I just said a blessing?"* At this point most (again about 80%) will say *"OK."* There is something about offering a "blessing" that allows you to pray for most people! At this point we go into our prayer that they would experience the love of God right there in the market place. If they said yes to the prayer and gave a request we pray that too.

The Importance of Consistency

One of the most critical elements of doing a prayer booth in the community is to do it on a consistent basis. You might have some success doing a one-time event, but the real fruit from this ministry is based on being present in the same place at the same time on a regular schedule. We find that a weekly schedule works well, as people remember that you are at a certain location on a specific day of the week. People will see you as a regular presence in the community, and that commitment will communicate your earnestness to be a blessing to that community. We have had countless people remark that they had driven past the prayer booth several times on that day of the week, some for months, before stopping. They report that God had been knocking on their heart every time they passed by. We also see return "customers," as people come back on future weeks or months to report what God has done or to receive more prayer. The only way that will happen is if you are at the same location at the same time in the future.

Prayer Exchange Journal

We use a simple journal to record the date and place of the prayer, the name of the person prayed for, and a brief summary of what was requested and prayed, along with any results. This serves several purposes, the most important being that if the person returns at a later date you can see what was prayed (and a reminder of their name!). This also communicates care to the individual, as there is a record of his or her last visit.

Doing a Co-Op

Some groups or individuals find it difficult to commit to being at the booth every week. Because weekly consistency is so important, we have found that one way to maintain this is to Co-Op with other groups or churches. We have one booth that we rotate in four different small groups within our church (home groups, bible studies, singles ministry, etc.) once a month. That way people get to participate in the outreach, but only have to commit to a monthly time slot. We also do another booth at a street fair where we rotate in different churches each month. Each church sends 3 to 4 people on their assigned month. (They can rotate in 3 to 4 people every 90 minutes if they have more that want to get involved.) We train each group as it comes in the first time so that we have continuity in our ethos (loving people, not pushing, praying that they will experience the love and power of Jesus, etc.). This is a great way to build unity among the churches in a city as we share the privilege of blessing those whom God sends us in the streets.

Going Fishing

When folks consider joining us to pray for people at the prayer booth, we always tell them to be prepared to wait (especially on the road side venues). The best analogy is that of going fishing. You usually don't go fishing for 30 minutes. You spend at least part of a day on a fishing trip! We set up the tent and put out the signs, and then we wait for God to draw people in for prayer. In a 3-hour session we average between 2 to 10 prayer exchanges at the road side and at times we may wait for over an hour before we get someone. (At the marketplace you will tend to get many more.) Be prepared to spend some time with "a line in the water" and enjoy the experience. (I like to bring my ukulele and sing!) Some days you get a few bites, and some you get many. And every once in a while you get to bring in a whopper (salvation, major healing, deliverance, etc.)!

Sample Prayer

We try to tailor the prayer for the individual based on need and spiritual condition (trying to determine that in a one minute interview is a challenge). Yet there are elements of the prayer that remain consistent regardless of for whom we pray. These elements are:

1. The love of God for that person.

2. The call of God for them to live in that love.

3. A request that they experience God's presence in that very moment.

If we were praying for Sandra with the request for a job, the prayer might go like this:

"Heavenly Father, I thank you for bringing Sandra to the prayer booth today, and giving her the courage to stop and let some

people pray for her. Lord, we ask that You would provide the right job for Sandra and to open a door that no one can shut. I thank You that You care for her so much, and that she is Your beloved daughter, whom You love. I ask that she would experience Your love and power right now in this place. Give her a greater revelation of Your purpose for her life, and let her know You are for her and with her always. I pray this in Jesus name, Amen."

Note – If we have a team (2 to 3 is recommended), each can take a turn praying, but we are conscious of keeping it brief. We pray for God's love and power to come regardless of whether people asking for prayer have indicated that they are a follower of Jesus or not. We are dependent on the Holy Spirit to draw them to the booth to get prayer, and we are also dependent on Him to reveal the love of the Father. We have found that teams larger than three or four tend to inhibit people from coming to get prayer. It's hard to share a need in a larger group, so many will not stop. If you have the good problem of having too many people who want to help pray, rotate them in on a schedule.

The Follow-up Question

This step is critical, and should not be skipped if at all possible! Ask this or a similar question:

"What were you experiencing while we were praying for you?"

This gives them a chance to put into words the work of the Holy Spirit in that short time we prayed for them. (They might not even recognize this as the Holy Spirit!) You will often be surprised by what they report! It can range from simple statements like *"I felt peace,"* or *"It was nice,"* to more profound responses like *"I felt tremendous heat on my body,"* or *"It felt like God was here!"* Some who have not been followers of Jesus have said things like *"I felt God say to me that I need to start listening to Him,"* or *"Something happened inside me today that I've never felt before – I don't know what it is."*

152

This feedback gives us insight into what God has been doing in the prayer exchange. We need to be gentle at this point and not be too pushy. As we are directed by the Spirit we can lead them to the next step with God (salvation, further healing, referral to a church if they don't already have one, etc.). This is all done without putting any guilt or *"You need to do this!"* being communicated. They must be willing, and cannot be pushed or coerced.

We also invite them to come back in the future (the importance of consistency) to report what God has been doing in their lives, or to get more prayer. They will often bring friends or family members in the weeks to come. This return serves not only to encourage us a pray-ers, but gives the recipients the opportunity to exercise the gift of thankfulness and gratitude.

Physical Healing

God wants to demonstrate His love and power through healing the sick. We have learned as we have prayed for more and more people to ask them if they have any physical or medical issues for which we can pray. Even if they have come to ask for some other prayer (a job, a crisis, or even to pray that their car passes the smog check!), we often ask, *"Do you have any health concerns or medical problems we can pray for?"* This seems to be even more effective with those who are not yet following Jesus. A short, specific prayer for healing can often result in tremendous results. It just seems that there is a great anointing for healing on the streets! We have lately seen cancer healed, severe arthritis removed, and several backs fully cured, and that is just the tip of the iceberg. Ask people who come in if you can pray for physical healing (even if you don't feel gifted in this area), and you will be surprised with what God wants to do. Go for it!

Summary

A *Prayer Booth* is a simple, yet profound way to do an outreach in your community. It is one of the many creative ways that God is leading the church to bring His love and power into the streets and the marketplace. Imagine the possibility of seeing hundreds of "Need Prayer?" Booths in cities and towns across the nation and all over the world! What might God do if we follow Him by offering simple yet powerful prayer in this way? Is God calling you to take a risk and do this too? We can say with confidence that if you persevere you will see the Kingdom of God break in with love and power, as lives are changed, healed, and set free. In the famous line from *The Water Boy*, "You can do it!"

Appendix A

Need Prayer? Booth Kit (what you need)

EZ-up type portable shelter (canopy) - A canopy will give you a place to hang banners and provide protection from sun and rain. We use the EZ-up type pop-ups (8x8 or 10x10), but just about anyone will work. (Slant legs work better for stability). You might find one cheap on Craigslist, but check the canopy for holes and the frame for broken/bent/missing parts. Cost: new about $90. Used $40?

Sandbags for the canopy – You will definitely need sandbags at some point, because when the wind comes the shelter turns into a kite! I have used weight plates and cans filled with cement, but the sandbags made specifically for portable shelters are the only way to go for the long run. I fill each with about 25 lbs. of sand. Cost: about $40 for 4 on eBay.

Banners – This is the most important part of your kit and the most expensive. We started out with homemade banners and they look cheap and don't last. We now use 8x2 screen printed banners (3 – front and sides, back open) with grommets (ends and middle) and they last and last. Cost: may vary by printers, but generally for three you will pay about $75 for each banner.

Elastic ties for banners – You will need three for each banner (ends and middle). We use the black elastic loops with the ball on the end, (not bungee cords) to attach the banners to the shelter. We have found over time it is best not to attach the bottom of the banner – just let it hang. This keeps it from becoming a sail in the wind! Cost: $10 or less. (Check dollar stores for these.)

Folding Chairs – You will need about 4, so look for used chairs on Craigslist or at yard sales. Cost: new $40, used $10?

Notebook/Journal – Take something in which to record the prayer exchanges. We use a theme book. Cost: $1.

Recyclable shopping bag – Fill a bag with New Believer Bibles (English and Spanish), a tissue box, hand sanitizer and some breath mints. Total cost: $10.

Optional but recommended:

A-Frame Sidewalk Sign – This is helpful for visibility. You can make one out of plywood with hinges (heavy), or buy a plastic Sempo type prefab one (light but expensive). I have made them out of plastic saw horses as well. We made one that is reversible with English on one side and Spanish on the other. Cost: handmade $10. Prefab $70-100.

Note: Some of our friends have used just an A-frame sign and set it up on the street near benches or parks, and wait nearby and pray for anyone who comes. I even read about a pastor who sets up a small sign (folded index card) on his table at Starbucks that invites anyone for payer. The variations are endless!

Total cost is between $200 and $400 (assuming you have nothing on hand).

Appendix B

My Tribute to Bill Jackson (Eulogy)

After a long battle with kidney disease, my good friend and mentor Jax went home to be with Jesus on June 17, 2015. This book, or at least much of what is contained in this book, would never have happened if not for the influence and friendship I had with Jax. The following is my eulogy for him:

In the course of our lives, God will bring some special people to bless us. If He brings a teacher, a person who can impart a love for Jesus through the Bible and though practical ministry, we are blessed. If God brings a mentor, a Christ-like example who lives out of a deep well of relationship with the Lord and helps us follow that same path, we are blessed. If He brings us a friend, a best-friend, one you can share your joys and sorrows with, one with whom you can partner in ministry, you are very blessed. I have been abundantly blessed, because I have had all those people in my life, and they are all the same person – Jax!

Before I actually met Bill Jackson, I felt like I already knew him because when I read his book, "Quest for the Radical Middle", I said, "This guy is describing me. This is my journey and this is the kind of church I want to be part of." A few years later I found out that the Jacksons were moving from San Diego to Corona to be part of our church at the Inland Vineyard! And to top it off, Jax was going to lead a new school of ministry right at my home church. Not long after that, Jax and I were introduced and we went to lunch at a nearby Daphne's restaurant. As we talked, I remember whispering a prayer "God, I really want to connect with this guy and learn from him." Little did I know how wonderfully the Lord would answer that prayer!

Jax had an amazing intellect, and his mind was overflowing in truth, wisdom and knowledge. I remember watching him in his office as he would type outlines on biblical or theological subjects from memory! As my professor at Trinity Learning Community and St. Stephens University, Jax was so full of knowledge and yet so full of the Spirit that it was at times overwhelming. Someone once described sitting under his teaching as "taking a drink from a firehose!" He was so enthusiastic about the Word, and so enthusiastic about the work of the Holy Spirit that I couldn't help being swept along for the ride. I was being caught up in the Grand Story of God, and Jax was helping me find my role in it. He was very encouraging, yet challenged me personally to become all that God had intended for me to be.

Not only did Jax teach me and become a mentor, but he brought me along as his partner in ministry. About this same time his health started going sideways. But it didn't seem to slow him down much, at least at first. There was about a four year period where we would travel together and do conferences in different cities. Jax used to jokingly call it the "B-level" circuit, where the big names in the Vineyard would travel the "A-level" circuit. He didn't care, and I was happy to be traveling and doing the work of ministry with my friend. He would teach and then do ministry even when the pain was crippling and his body was giving out. He testified that he saw more people healed in this last season of his life's ministry then the previous 25 years. Yet he was not physically healed himself even though he received prayer thousands of times. He was the embodiment of the "already and not yet" of the Kingdom. I still don't understand it and neither did Jax, but in the times we talked about it, he would say, "In the final analysis, you have to rest in the truth that God is good."

Most people knew Jax as a gifted teacher and a loving pastor, and I experienced those things from him in abundance. Yet the quality that sticks with me the most about his life is perseverance. He modeled long-suffering and endurance in ministry in a way that made me wonder – how does he do it? What keeps him going through the pain? He must have been drawing from a deeper well of knowing Jesus than most of us have yet to experience. He had a godly character that stood the test, and we who knew him are much the richer for it.

Jax, you have fought the good fight, you have finished the race, and you have kept the faith. Now there is in store for you the crown of righteousness given by the Lord Jesus. You will wear it well my friend.

About the Author

Todd W. Volker is an urban missionary, author and conference speaker. He started his professional career as a public school teacher for about 23 years before being called into the ministry. After graduation from St. Stephen's University with a Masters of Ministry degree, his calling took an interesting turn. Not a position as a pastor in a church, but a dedication to minister to ordinary people on the streets and in the marketplace. Since then he has prayed for thousands of people he has met in unique situations, from street markets to the crowds at MMA fighting events.
He is now helping to equip others to do the same sort of ministry: Taking the love and power of Jesus outside the walls of the church and into the streets and marketplace.
Todd has been married to his wife Pam for over 35 years, and they have two adult children, Joel and Bethany. His hobbies include collecting and restoring pinball machines and playing the ukulele.

You can reach Todd at:

todd@streetlevelprayer.com

Endorsements for *Street Level Prayer*

"There are a lot of books out there that are written with lofty theological ideas and platitudes - this is not one of those books. This is a how-to, get dirty, in the trenches, survivor's guide. *Street Level Prayer* is a book about living out the pages of scripture outside of the walls of our church buildings. It is written by someone who has already walked the walk and you can trust his talk. If impacting your community with the power of prayer is what you are looking for, this is the book you have been searching for - and it is the book that everyone should be reading."
-Trinity Jordan
Assistant United States Attorney for the Southern District of Florida; Founding Pastor of Elevation Church, Utah.

"Todd Volker's book, *Street Level Prayer*, describes a ministry approach that provides a good way of connecting with people in a spirit of love, availability and support. It's an especially outstanding resource for those who come from a tradition of Spirit-led demonstration of the power of God, as this book flows out of the classic Vineyard movement. Some of the aspects that are particularly helpful include a gracious spirit, a sense of humility, and openness to listening to the spirit of God in obedience as opposed to leading with your own agenda. Volker also addresses various questions and practical concerns people commonly wonder about with this type of ministry.

Yet even for those who don't come from a Vineyard theological background, if read with an open mind, *Street Level Prayer* can help all of us reflect on how we do ministry. How can we more fully engage and participate in the works of Jesus as Jesus said we would in John 14:12? How can we be a part of what God is doing and how can we make ourselves available to the community outside the walls of the church?"
-Dr. Bob Logan
Ministry coach and author of The Discipleship Difference

"*Street Level Prayer* is a must read for anyone that would like to learn to minister to others the way that Jesus did. Todd Volker Provides an intimate and informed guide for engaging people with the love and power of God. Todd, who was trained by Bill Jackson, who was trained by John Wimber, gives a naturally super natural approach to Street Level Prayer. Don't miss out on this practical and powerful book."
-Travis Twyman
Lead Pastor, Inland Vineyard Church

"I want to commend to you Todd Volker's new book, *Street Level Prayer*. For the last several years, Todd has been a leader in using prayer on the streets as an evangelistic strategy in Southern California. This book will walk you through his philosophy of ministry, and what makes for success and failure. If you have a heart for evangelism and for the supernatural in everyday life, this book will inspire and challenge you to go further."

-Ken Fish
Founder, Kingdom Fire Ministries

Todd's book is incredible! For anyone longing to learn to minister the love of Jesus in the streets, this is an incredible resource! I can attest personally to Todd's love for Jesus and his longing to see people come to know the King. Todd's taught me so much about prayer and loving people and I want to encourage you to grab this work and give it a read. He not only gives the larger context for praying for folks on the streets, but he also provides such helpful tips about walking this out. And on a more personal note, he writes an amazing eulogy for my Dad at the end as my Dad mentored Todd and played a crucial discipleship role in his life.

-Luc Jackson
Teacher, Preacher, Missionary

Made in United States
Troutdale, OR
08/25/2023

12372254R00105